DON'T LET ME BE LONELY

Also by Claudia Rankine

Poetry and Essays
Just Us: An American Conversation
Citizen: An American Lyric
Plot
The End of the Alphabet
Nothing in Nature Is Private

Plays
Help
The White Card
The Provenance of Beauty: A South Bronx Travelogue

Coeditor
The Racial Imaginary: Writers on Race in the Life of the Mind
American Poets in the 21st Century
American Women Poets in the 21st Century

DON'T LET ME BE LONELY

An American Lyric

Claudia Rankine

Graywolf Press

"All those sleep shapes" by Paul Celan from *Poems of Paul Celan*, translated by Michael Hamburger. Translation copyright © 1972, 1980, 1988, 2002 by Michael Hamburger. Reprinted by permission of Persea Books, Inc., New York.

"Gift" from *The Collected Poems 1931–1997* by Czeslaw Milosz. Copyright © 1988 by Czeslaw Milosz Royalties, Inc. Reprinted by permission of HarperCollins Publishers, Inc.

This publication is made possible, in part, by the voters of Minnesota through a Minnesota State Arts Board Operating Support grant, thanks to a legislative appropriation from the arts and cultural heritage fund. Significant support has also been provided by other generous contributions from foundations, corporations, and individuals. To these organizations and individuals we offer our heartfelt thanks.

MINNESOTA
STATE ARTS BOARD

CLEAN
WATER
LAND &
LEGACY
AMENDMENT

Published by Graywolf Press
212 Third Avenue North, Suite 485
Minneapolis, Minnesota 55401

First edition published 2004. Second edition published 2024.

www.graywolfpress.org

Published in the United States of America

ISBN 978-1-64445-255-4 (paperback)
ISBN 978-1-64445-256-1 (ebook)

2 4 6 8 9 7 5 3 1
First Graywolf Printing, 2024

Library of Congress Control Number: 2022952328

Cover design and photograph: John Lucas

And most of all beware, even in thought, of assuming the sterile attitude of the spectator, for life is not a spectacle, a sea of grief is not a proscenium, a man who wails is not a dancing bear . . .

AIMÉ CÉSAIRE

As soon as I *desire* I am asking to be considered. I am not merely here-and-now, sealed into thingness. I am for somewhere else and for something else. I demand that notice be taken of my negating activity insofar as I pursue something other than life; insofar as I do battle for the creation of a human world—that is, of a world of reciprocal recognitions.

He who is reluctant to recognize me opposes me. In a savage struggle I am willing to accept convulsions of death, invincible dissolution, but also the possibility of the impossible.

FRANTZ FANON

For Ula Alexandra Lucas

Preface

I first began working on *Don't Let Me Be Lonely* in Paris in 1999 during the run-up to the turn of the millennium and the George W. Bush presidency. It was my sabbatical year from Barnard College and I was living in the Southwest of London. That fall, in Paris for a long weekend, I remember strolling by a café table and reaching out for a paper napkin in order to write down some thoughts. By the time I returned to our rented house on Whittlesey Street near Waterloo Station, I was writing in a notebook what seemed to me to be episodic meditations on what it means to live simultaneously in community and in isolation.

I deliberately wrote from a position of incomplete knowing and understanding, not knowing exactly but feeling completely. I allowed hesitancy, worry, fear, apprehension, and need to be my subjects wherever I saw, heard, or felt any or all of these emotions. The pieces became a collection of movements in the historical present that I witnessed in my own life and in the lives of others in both very public and very private arenas. I went from thinking about the pieces as meditations on events to laments in real time. Eventually, I began to understand the writing as emotional expressions of moments in time and not so much records of a singular life. These were lyrics holding historical affect. Loneliness and violence were flooding our days, or so I felt. Fear was driving both our actions and stasis. For some of us, the fear was an excuse for cruelty, and for others, fear was synonymous with terror. Loss was the same as it ever was.

It is an understatement to say that *Lonely* was a watershed moment for me as a writer at that time. As I sat in my office on the second floor of what was once a dockworker's home in Lambeth by the Thames, I knew the new work differed from my three previously published books. The same training that produced those books informed this new project, with one difference: I wasn't self-consciously experimenting with the possibilities of language; I was consciously representing a world as I both saw and felt it, and therefore, the bullshit notion that politics have no place in poems had to be understood as self-erasure. To write, while fully knowing, seeing, and feeling, meant I needed to take what was needed formally and theoretically from the two dominant poetry traditions of the time and let the rest go.

To oversimplify, I will say I was positioned between the theory-driven Language poetry and the tradition of inward-turning writing often described as overheard emotion. The contemporary white writers dominating the poetry landscape at the end of the twentieth century neither saw that their whiteness was political nor that the world was dedicated to their white supremacy. Consequently, it was beyond their abilities to understand how their whiteness informed their writing and their poetics; most maintained a level of uneducated, willful unconsciousness that made little sense but held all the power. This was true on both sides of the aesthetic divide within the two dominant poetic communities but in different ways. (I felt this in part because I had co-chaired a conference with Professor Allison Cummings at Barnard entitled "Where Lyric Tradition Meets Language Poetry: Innovation in Contemporary American Poetry by Women," in April 1999, in an attempt to address how siloed and segregated both communities were, on and off the page.) My intention was for *Lonely* to put pressure on the dominant lyric model while holding onto the modes of writing that made apparent the power structures inherent in language use underlined by some of the work of the Language poets. I also was interested in attaching affective frequencies or a grammar of interiority to some of the Language poets' more theoretical approach of the Language poets.

In as much as *Lonely* has a backdrop, it is New York City under the mayorship of Rudolph Giuliani at the change of the millennium. The Supreme Court had inserted itself in the 2000 election by overturning a state law requiring a recount in Florida where an illegally narrow margin of 537 votes awarded the state for Bush, thus handing him Florida's twenty-five electoral votes and the presidency. If the Supreme Court had seemed a safeguard of our democratic practices, I regarded it quite differently after that election, given the infrequency with which a president won without the popular vote, a dynamic that would be repeated in the election of Donald Trump in 2016.

When the clock struck midnight to start 2000, the Y2K problem was solved with a four-digit number. The fear and terror that had built our American culture would broaden in scope with the 9/11 attacks and the destruction of the World Trade Center in 2001. The obvious misinformation circulated by the Bush Administration and peddled by the Fourth Estate in our rising forms of new digital media eroded any trust in journalism and our understanding of facts. The writer Susan Sontag would point this out in an essay in the *New Yorker* regarding America's response to 9/11:

> The voices licensed to follow the event seem to have joined together in a campaign to infantilize the public. Where is the acknowledgment that this was not a "cowardly" attack on "civilization" or "liberty" or "humanity" or "the free world" but an attack on the world's self-proclaimed superpower,

undertaken as a consequence of specific American alliances and actions? How many citizens are aware of the ongoing American bombing of Iraq? And if the word "cowardly" is to be used, it might be more aptly applied to those who kill from beyond the range of retaliation, high in the sky, than to those willing to die themselves in order to kill others.

On May 19, 2022, former president Bush would inadvertently agree with Sontag in an attempt to condemn Vladimir Putin's war on Ukraine: "The result is an absence of checks and balances in Russia, and the decision of one man to launch a wholly unjustified and brutal invasion of Iraq—I mean of Ukraine."

This realm of media-world-building ultimately determined the structural form of *Lonely*. The oversized vertical format and black-and-white images of the original publication in 2004 were meant to speak back to newspaper columns and opinion pieces. The new edition, published twenty years later, has moved into full color to acknowledge the shift to online media with an updated screen that functions both as television and computer screen. The present importance of the documentary image captured and circulated by phone has informed the replacement of some illustrations in the text, though many original illustrations remain.

The use of the first person throughout *Lonely* is a strategy I came to in an attempt to maintain a form of intimacy and agility within the prose poems themselves. The first person seemed more a rudder than an authentic self as I had been schooled to believe it should be by the traditional lyric. The agility and fungibility of a single subjectivity allowed the voice of these pieces to roam the landscape of the book's experiences, which exist beyond the experiences of my own life. "I" was there to signal a disembodied speaker in the sense that it could inhabit multiple bodies experiencing or looking on or being alongside. To answer a question of the poet Paul Celan, "I" was there to bear witness to the witness. I, Claudia, was not the woman on the roof, but there was a woman on a roof having the experiences that we as readers step into. Anybody could embody the first person and be our guide through the text. For me, at the time, this was a liberating mechanism for getting at the ineffable affective disorder of the moment without disconnecting from the people affected by it. "I" was able to exist within everyone's quotidian, the one I knew intimately, the one in the television, the one running for office, the one documenting the moments, the one running the country, the one in books, and so on.

The added notes were placed at the end of the book to underline the lyric nature of the pieces. *Lonely* was fictive though everything had happened. The notes held the facts as they were known at the time. I wanted to separate the affective orientation from the factual information. No attempt was made to correct memory in the body of the text. Someone said this thing. Someone did this thing. I wanted to follow them emotionally, not factually. Affect forms within the feeling of what we feel we know. How we enter the generalized experience is mostly partial and episodic. In the end, because we are here together, our private feelings are informed atmospherically and grounded in our collective chronic conditions. How we give shape to the memory of that might not be factual, but its shapes inform the truth of the feeling and of the times. The notes reinforce an acknowledgment or a recognition within the body of the text that there is always more to know or another way of knowing or no other way forward for memory. *Lonely* was a stand-alone collection until it wasn't. When Graywolf asked me to frame the title, I wished to underline the political nature of being as "being itself" within the writing of poetry. There is no outside of the politics that shape the quotidian. The fact that white people presented their lyric poetry as beyond politics was itself political. The poet Richard Howard had referred to the poems in *Lonely* as "lyrics" in a note he wrote in support of the original manuscript, and my own desire to firmly embed them in our history of white supremacy and capitalism necessitated the addition of "American." *Don't Let Me Be Lonely: An American Lyric* was followed ten years later in 2014 by *Citizen: An American Lyric* and finally in 2020 by *Just Us: An American Conversation.* The trilogy taken as a whole covers the time from 1999 to 2020, more than two decades of violence and hatred in an increasingly divided nation under the leadership of presidents Bush, Obama, and Trump. Following the 2010 antigovernment protests in the Arab world known as the Arab Spring, protest movements like Occupy Wall Street, Black Lives Matter, and #MeToo all insisted on a more integrated and accountable assessment of America's anti-Black, misogynist, white supremacist, patriarchal, and capitalist impact on our daily lives. Following *Lonely, Citizen* and *Just Us* attempt to both reflect and forge conversations in light of our daily struggles with the power structures limiting our possibilities and reframing our realities. Many readers came to the trilogy through the door opened by *Citizen*'s publication. The reissue of *Lonely* is a look back at where the concept of the "American Lyric" actually begins.

Claudia Rankine

DON'T LET ME BE LONELY

There was a time I could say no one I knew well had died. This is not to suggest no one died. When I was eight my mother became pregnant. She went to the hospital to give birth and returned without the baby. Where's the baby? we asked. Did she shrug? She was the kind of woman who liked to shrug; deep within her was an everlasting shrug. That didn't seem like a death. The years went by and people only died on television—if they weren't Black, they were wearing black or were terminally ill. Then I returned home from school one day and saw my father sitting on the steps of our home. He had a look that was unfamiliar; it was flooded, so leaking. I climbed the steps as far away from him as I could get. He was breaking or broken. Or, to be more precise, he looked to me like someone under-standing his aloneness. Loneliness. His mother was dead. I'd never met her. It meant a trip back home for him. When he returned he spoke neither about the airplane nor the funeral.

Every movie I saw while in the third grade compelled me to ask, Is he dead? Is she dead? Because the characters often live against all odds it is the actors whose mortality concerned me. If it were an old, black-and-white film, whoever was around would answer yes. Months later the actor would show up on some late-night talk show to promote his latest efforts. I would turn and say—one always turns to say—You said he was dead. And the misinformed would claim, I never said he was dead. Yes, you did. No, I didn't. Inevitably we get older; whoever is still with us says, Stop asking me that.

Or one begins asking oneself that same question differently. Am I dead? Though this question at no time explicitly translates into Should I be dead, eventually the suicide hotline is called. You are, as usual, watching television, the eight-o'clock movie, when a number flashes on the screen: 1–800–SUICIDE. You dial the number. Do you feel like killing yourself? the man on the other end of the receiver asks. You tell him, I feel like I am already dead. When he makes no response you add, I am in death's position. He finally says, Don't believe what you are thinking and feeling. Then he asks, Where do you live?

Fifteen minutes later the doorbell rings. You explain to the ambulance attendant that you had a momentary lapse of happily. The noun, happiness, is a static state of some Platonic ideal you know better than to pursue. Your modifying process had happily or unhappily experienced a momentary pause. This kind of thing happens, perhaps is still happening. He shrugs and in turn explains that you need to come quietly or he will have to restrain you. If he is forced to restrain you, he will have to report that he is forced to restrain you. It is this simple: Resistance will only make matters more difficult. Any resistance will only make matters worse. By law, I will have to restrain you. His tone suggests that you should try to understand the difficulty in which he finds himself. This is further disorienting. I am fine! Can't you see that! You climb into the ambulance unassisted.

Or say the eyes are resting when the phone rings and what this friend wants to tell you is that in five years she will be dead. She says simply, I have breast cancer. Then in the incredulous tone she uses to refer to strange behavior by boyfriends and coworkers, she adds, Do you believe this? Can you believe this? Can you?

The lump was misdiagnosed a year earlier. Can we say she might have lived had her doctor not screwed up? If yes—when does her death actually occur?

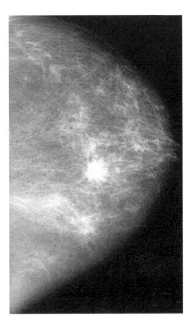

During the mastectomy she has muscle mass and some fatty something or other removed from her abdominal area and used in the reconstruction of her left breast. The plastic surgeon argued she could do a far better job with natural versus artificial tissue. It added an extra day to her hospital stay.

After the mastectomy, the chemotherapy, the radiation, and the waiting, we learn the cancer is in this friend's bones and know it is settled. I go to see her two months before she dies. Her skin by then reveals her skeleton. It is easy for the eyes not to stare, easy to accept the fact that the cancer has been replaced by the approach of death. It is easy to accept that her personality has been overshadowed by its condition, that the condition, her death, has imprinted itself. No second look is necessary.

Cancer slowly settled in her body and lived off it until it, her body, became useless to itself. A hell of a way to lose weight, she says when I step into her bedroom and take the look that becomes the unforgettable imprint. We watch a lot of television the four days I sit at her bedside. We talk. She grows tired. She is sad. She grows tired. She becomes angry. She grows tired. She is accepting. She grows tired. She grows tired.

As I look around the room, which is packed with her possessions, moved months before into her mother's home, any lingering interest in any object or piece of clothing is interrupted—

She explains to me that the "Do-not-resuscitate" (DNR) sign merely means no cardiopulmonary resuscitation (CPR). Even if I could, I am not allowed to administer chest compressions, insert an artificial airway, administer resuscitative drugs, defibrillate, cardiovert, or initiate cardiac monitoring. No. No. No. No. No. She has decided. She's grown tired. She is finished. No matter whose will to life remains at her bedside, her death is safe.

One night we discuss at great length the movies *Boogie Nights* and *Magnolia*. The consensus is that both movies are motivated by the theme of the disappointing father figure. In both movies men old enough to be anybody's father do bad things to people who are younger than they are, people who could be their children, people who are their children, people who if these father figures had behaved better could have looked up to them for the slimmest of reasons. Tom Cruise is convincing as the disappointed son in *Magnolia*. There is another character with my same name who is also bitterly disappointed. Though the subject of cancer did not come up in our late-night conversation about the two movies, it did for him, for Tom Cruise's character in *Magnolia*.

Why do people waste away? The fact that cancer describes a malignant mass of tissue that pulls all nutrients from the body surprises the body first, then the owner of the body, and finally those who look on. Or as Gertrude Stein, who herself died of stomach cancer, points out, "if everybody did not die the earth would be all covered over and I, I as I, could not have come to be and try as much as I can try not to be I, nevertheless, I would mind that so much, as much as anything, so then why not die, and yet and again not a thing, not a thing to be liking, not a thing."

I leave the television on all the time. It faces the empty bed. I don't go into the bedroom during the day once I've dressed. Sometimes when I am wearing a skirt and feel like putting on pants or vice versa, I go in there and people are conversing. Occasionally I sit on the edge of the bed and listen. I listen for a few minutes only. One day there is a man interviewing a boy caught in the penal system, a juvenile offender—

Man: *He is deceased?*
Boy: *He is dead to me.*
Man: *So he is not deceased?*
Boy: *I don't know. He could be dead.*
Man: *Is he or is he not dead?*
Boy: *He's been dead to my life.*
Man: *Someone wrote in your file that he is dead. Did you tell someone he is dead?*
Boy: *All right, he is dead.*

umm pa pa

That day I find I can't work, so in the margin of my note-
book I write a dialogue.

    I thought I was dead.

    You thought you were dead?

    I thought I was.

    Did you feel dead?

    I said, God rest me.

    God rest your soul?

    I thought I was dead.

    You tried everything?

    I waited.

    You spoke aloud?

    I said, God rest me.

    You'd let me be lonely?

    I thought I was dead.

Or say a friend develops Alzheimer's. For a while he understands he is getting ill and will die within this illness. On a slate message board in his house, he writes

He is moved to a home: Manor Care. Then he becomes violent and is moved to another home: Fairlawn. All this takes five years. Then he dies. I bring the chalkboard home with me and hang it on the wall in my study. Whenever I look up from my desk it is there—

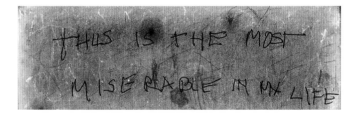

One day I hear, as if he is standing next to me, the poet Joseph Brodsky saying, *What's the point of forgetting if it's followed by dying?* Joseph Brodsky is dead, but this fact does not stop his voice from entering the room every time I look up—this is the most miserable in my life *what's the point of forgetting if it's followed by dying* this is the most miserable in my life *what's the point . . .* I can't stop people from saying what they need to say. I don't know how to stop repetitions like these.

The chalkboard has a built-in ledge, on the ledge is an eraser, but he scratched in the words

with some sort of sharp edge.

When his memory started to go, he substituted a kind of makeshift reality. He developed the irritation of a three-year-old fighting his way to a sentence. One day he pointed to the television and with great effort and concentration finally said, I want to see the lady who deals in death. The first time you hear him say this, you think his condition has given him insight into his own mortality. The phrase echoes in your head, The lady who deals in death. The lady who deals in death. The lady who deals in death. The lady who deals. Until, finally, *Murder, She Wrote*.

Cornel West makes the point that hope is different from American optimism. After the initial presidential election results come in, I stop watching the news. I want to continue watching, charting, and discussing the counts, the recounts, the hand counts, but I cannot. I lose hope. However Bush came to have won, he would still be winning ten days later and we would still be in the throes of our American optimism. All the non-reporting is a distraction from Bush himself, the same Bush who can't remember if two or three people were convicted for dragging a Black man to his death in his home state of Texas.

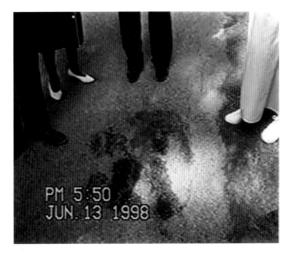

You don't remember because you don't care. Sometimes my mother's voice swells and fills my forehead. Mostly I resist the flooding, but in Bush's case I find myself talking to the television screen: *You don't know because you don't care.*

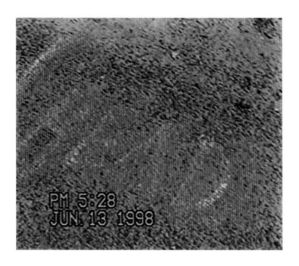

Then, like all things impassioned, this voice takes on a life of its own: *You don't know because you don't bloody care. Do you?*

I forget things too. It makes me sad. Or it makes me the saddest. The sadness is not really about George W. or our American optimism; the sadness lives in the recognition that a life can not matter. Or, as there are billions of lives, my sadness is alive alongside the recognition that billions of lives never mattered. I write this without breaking my heart, without bursting into anything. Perhaps this is the real source of my sadness. Or, perhaps, Emily Dickinson, my love, hope was never a thing with feathers. I don't know, I just find when the news comes on I switch the channel. This new tendency might be indicative of a deepening personality flaw: IMH, The Inability to Maintain Hope, which translates into no innate trust in the supreme laws that govern us. Cornel West says this is what is wrong with Black people today—too nihilistic. Too scarred by hope to hope, too experienced to experience, too close to dead is what I think.

There is a button on the remote control called FAV. You can program your favorite channels. Don't like the world you live in, choose one closer to the world you live in. I choose the independent film channel and HBO. Neither have news programs as far as I can tell. This is what is great about America—anyone can make these kinds of choices. Instead of the news, HBO has *The Sopranos*. This week the indie channel is playing and replaying Spaghetti Westerns. Always someone gets shot or pierced through the heart with an arrow, and just before he dies he says, I am not going to make it. Where? Not going to make it where? On some level, maybe, the phrase simply means not going to make it into the next day, hour, minute, or perhaps the next second. Occasionally, you can imagine, it means he is not going to make it to Carson City or Texas or somewhere else out west or to Mexico if he is on the run. On another level always implicit is the sense that it means he is not going to make it to his own death. Perhaps in the back of all our minds is the life expectancy for our generation. Perhaps this expectation lingers there alongside the hours of sleep one should get or the number of times one is meant to chew food—eight hours, twenty chews, and seventy-six years. We are all heading there and not to have that birthday is not to have made it.

Peckinpah's *The Wild Bunch* is worth watching because the cowboys in it have nowhere to get to. They're older and they don't have to make it anywhere because where they are is all there is or rather the end of a genre. Theirs is not the Old Testament—no journey to take; nothing promised; no land to land in. For them, life and death are simultaneously equal and present. The simultaneity of the living who are already dead is filmed as sexy.

Peckinpah gives the final shoot-out in which they all die a kind of orgasmic rush that releases all of us from the cinematic or, more accurately, the American fantasy that we will survive no matter what. Though they are handsome, white, leading men not dressed all in black, he literally shoots the life out of all anticipatory leanings. Once the orgasm is over we can just lie back, close our eyes, and relax, though we are neither liberated nor fulfilled. In our own "little deaths" we understand that once they are dead, we are finished, no American fantasy can help us now.

In the night I watch television to help me fall asleep, or I watch television because I cannot sleep. My husband sleeps through my sleeplessness and the noise of the television. Eventually it is all a blur. I never remember turning the TV off, but always when I wake up in the morning, it is off. Perhaps he turns it off. I don't know.

Some nights I count the commercials for antidepressants. If the same commercial is repeated, I still count it. It seems right that pharmaceutical companies should advertise in the middle of the night, when people are less distracted and capable of tuning in more and more and most precisely to their fearful bodies and their accompanying anxieties.

One commercial for PAXIL (paroxetine HCI) says simply: YOUR LIFE IS WAITING. Parataxis, I think first, but then I wonder, for what, for what does it wait? For life I guess.

Across the screen, this time minus audio, flashes:

It remains on the screen long enough so that when I close my eyes to check if I am sleeping, instead of darkness, YOURLIFEISWAITING stares back at me.

The commercial for another drug says, Take these pills.
If you get a certain set of side effects (I won't enumerate),
you can take this other pill in addition.

Some Medicines Can Change The Effect
Of This Medicine. Check With Your
Doctor Or Pharmacist Before Taking Any
Other Medicines.

The woman on the television screen is smiling. I cannot
help but think her results are not typical.

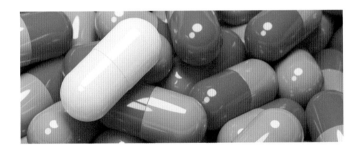

The prescription the doctor writes me says, Take one pill every day before going to sleep.

By the fifteenth day it's clear it isn't working. Take two a day then, she says. In a week there are no more pills. She writes a new prescription. The pharmacist refuses to fill it.

You should still have seven pills. The insurance company won't cover this.

She said take two a day.

They always do that.

Call my doctor.

She can't change the authorization.

The authorization? Oh.

Come back tomorrow.

The next day he tries again. Again it doesn't work, and then it does. He gives me the pills. It is unclear what changes, but I take the pills.

No bag.

Or she says, You might not need these pills, but if it turns out you need them, you want to have them close by.

Close by are the pills. They are red, each bigger than a Tic Tac, smaller than a kidney bean.

> a. It turns out I decide not to take them.
> b. I put them in the bathroom cabinet.
> c. I never touch them.
> d. Sometimes I open the cabinet.
> e. I see the plastic container.
> f. The red pills catch my eye.
> g. I take the container off the shelf.
> h. I read my name.
> i. I read the instructions.
> j. I rub my thumb over the typed letters.
> k. I never open the safety cap.

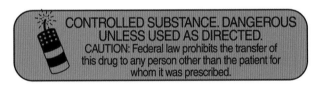

CONTROLLED SUBSTANCE. DANGEROUS UNLESS USED AS DIRECTED. CAUTION: Federal law prohibits the transfer of this drug to any person other than the patient for whom it was prescribed.

My desire is to give the pills away as I might a pair of shoes I have never worn. I want to give them to a friend, to someone who could decide to throw them away.

The day is hot, unbearably. The lack of air-conditioning persuades a girl up to the roof of her thirty-story apartment building despite the sign in bold letters, TENANTS NOT ALLOWED ON ROOF. She is not afraid of heights. The water tower casts shade just big enough for her torso. To keep her calves out of the sun and off the hot roof she lets them hang over the edge of the building.

The sky is drowning in blue with clouds that billow like sails, a blue sea of sails. After a while of just lying there, the girl decides to shout a Milosz poem to the sky.

A day so happy
Fog lifted early, I worked in the garden.
Hummingbirds were stopping over honeysuckle flowers.
There was no thing on earth I wanted to possess.
I knew no one worth my envying him.
Whatever evil I had suffered, I forgot.
To think that once I was the same man did not embarrass me.
In my body I felt no pain.
When straightening up, I saw the blue sea and sails.

Even if she could hear the ambulances, why would she take them personally? Milosz said that America was a land of great loneliness. She came outside to get away from that.

A crowd gathers below. Had she known people could see her from their apartments across the street, see her calves, her size-seven feet, her green nail-polished toes, she would have gone back inside despite the heat.

Then, as if she is dreaming, she hears a woman almost whispering call her honey. Honey, what's your name? comes softly from behind her. Luckily, she doesn't startle. Everything will be all right, the police officer says. The girl lifts her legs over the edge; she stands. Two other officers appear from behind the heavy door. The girl's confusion is genuine, and therefore should be convincing. Nonetheless, she has to go to the hospital for tests, which translate into someone asking her a few questions along the lines of, Are you okay?

The strange thing is that before they take her to the hospital, the ambulance stops at the police station. At the station the sergeant is or is not interested but he does ask, What the hell do you think you were doing? The girl loves him for asking. She loves him for keeping her thinking in the present even as her actions dissolve into our past. In all our dreams his question is the question that stays.

The Museum of Emotions in London has a game that asks *yes* and *no* questions. As long as you answer "correctly," you can continue playing. The third question is: Were you terribly upset and did you find yourself weeping when Princess Diana died?

I told the truth and stepped on the NO tile. I was not allowed to continue. The museum employee, who must have had a thing with shame, looked away as I stepped down. Walking out, I couldn't help but think the question should have been, Was Princess Diana ever really alive? I mean, alive to anyone outside of her friends and family—truly?

The English were very distraught after her death. On the television they showed thousands of mourners leaving flowers in front of the palace.

Weren't they mourning the protection they felt she should have had? A protection they'll never have? Weren't they simply grieving the random inevitability of their own lives?

My mother tells me I am just biding time. She means it as a push toward not biding time. She wants me to lead a readable life—one that can be read as worthwhile, and successful. My mother is not overly concerned with happiness, its fruitless pursuit or otherwise. As far as she can remember, there was only pain connected to the joy of childbirth. She remembers the pain and wants it to have been worthwhile, for a reasonable life.

As I watch my mother's mouth move, I ask myself: Am I often troubled by constipation? Have I ever vomited love or coughed up blame? Is anything wrong with my mind?

A father tells his son the thing he regrets most about his life is the amount of time he has spent worrying about it.

Worry 1. A dog's action of biting and shaking an animal so as to injure or kill it, spec., a hound's worrying of its quarry; an instance of this. 2. A state or feeling of mental unease or anxiety regarding or arising from one's cares or responsibilities, uncertainty about the future, fear of failure, etc.; anxious concern, anxiety. Also, an instance or cause of this.

It achieved nothing, all his worrying. Things worked out or they didn't work out and now here he was, an old man, an old man who each year of his life bit or shook doubt as if to injure if not to kill, an old man with a good-looking son who resembles his deceased mother. It is uncanny how she rests there, as plain as day, in their boy's face.

Worry 8. Cause mental distress or agitation to (a person, oneself); make anxious and ill at ease. 9. Give way to anxiety, unease, or disquietude: allow one's mind to dwell on difficulties or troubles.

He waits for his father's death. His father has been taken off the ventilator and clearly will not be able to breathe for himself much longer. Earlier in the day the nurse mentioned something about an electroencephalogram (EEG), which measures brain waves in the cerebral hemispheres, the parts of the brain that deal with speech and memory. But his brain stem is damaged; it seems now the test will not be necessary. The son expects an almost silent, hollow gasp to come from the old man's open mouth. Those final sounds, however, are nothing like the wind moving through the vacancy of a mind. The release is jerky and convulsive. There is never the rasp or the choke the son expects, though one meaning of worry is to be choked on, to choke on.

Or last year this close friend was in the depression of his life. He had to take a medical leave from his job as a speech-writer. He could barely get out of bed. That's what he said so he might have meant he wasn't getting out of bed. He said he felt like an old man dying, the old man dying. The leaves on the trees outside his window rattled within him.

Before his breakdown, we had DVD evenings. I'd go over with a bag of Doritos and a bottle of wine. After the break-down, he didn't wish to see anyone. He wasn't answering the phone. I called; I left messages—sometimes to break into the general silence and sometimes to check on him. Finally, he agreed I should come by. I walked the thirty-six blocks to his apartment. By the time I reached his place I was anxious but optimistic. I thought the apartment would be a mess; the apartment was dust free. He seemed fine.

We sat on the sofa in front of his television. He crossed his legs and seemed excessively silent, though I had no real grounds for comparison having never noticed the quality of his small talk before. He had rented *Fitzcarraldo* from Movie Place. They pick up and deliver. Herzog is his favor-ite director. He refused the glass of wine I poured for him.

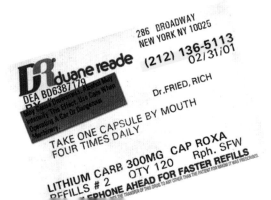

His body couldn't take alcohol and drugs at the same time. He was on Lithium, one capsule four times daily. There was a red sticker on his medicine bottle warning against alcohol use. He handed me the bottle.

While watching the movie, tears rolled down his cheeks. Apart from their use in expressing emotion, tears have two other functions: they lubricate the eyes so that the lids can move over them smoothly as you blink; they wash away foreign bodies. It is difficult to feel much tear-worthy emotion about anything in *Fitzcarraldo* as it is about having outlandish projects and achieving them in the name of art, but since the tears kept coming long after smooth blinking would have been restored and foreign bodies washed away, I decided that apparently my friend was expressing emotion and was not fine, not okay, no.

Timothy McVeigh died at 7:14 a.m. and a news reporter asks relatives of his 168 victims if they have forgiven him. Perhaps because McVeigh is visually the American boy next door, this is yet another attempt by the media to immunize him from his actions. Still it is unclear to me why the reporter asks this now, but I nonetheless continue watching to hear what is said. Many say, No, no, I have not forgiven him. A few say, Yes.

What does it mean to forgive and how does forgiveness show itself? "Forgiveness forgives only the unforgivable," Jacques Derrida claims. Timothy McVeigh never asked to be forgiven. He managed to suggest that both condemnation and forgiveness were irrelevant by quoting William Earnest Henley's poem "Invictus": "It matters not how strait the gate, How charged with punishments the scroll, I am the master of my fate: I am the captain of my soul." The need for forgiveness does not seem to enter into McVeigh's final statement to the media. Even as his judicial execution by lethal injection is televised over closed-circuit television for the victims' families, he makes no sign that forgiveness is necessary to him.

So what is forgiveness and how does it show itself?

Forgiveness, I finally decide, is not the death of amnesia, nor is it a form of madness, as Derrida claims. For the one who forgives, it is simply a death, a dying down in the heart, the position of the already dead. It is in the end the living through, the understanding that this has happened, is happening, happens. Period. It is a feeling of nothingness that cannot be communicated to another, an absence, a bottomless vacancy held by the living, beyond all that is hated or loved.

That same night I dream the Kennedys invite me to a party. All the Kennedys who are dead are dead. Caroline is there and she speaks very nicely to me—is very gracious. Though one can go three days without water and survive, I have a few glasses of Perrier with lemon, mill around, have a fine time. When I am ready to leave, the waiter, a camel at his side, comes forward with the bill. I take out ten dollars, but all those glasses of water add up to ten thousand dollars. Pardon me, I say to the waiter. I am, obviously, caught unprepared both financially and contextually.

I was switched from Prozac to fluoxetine. Prozac's patent is up, and now that the generic brand, fluoxetine, is available, the insurance company will only cover that, my editor says casually. Because talk shows and reality TV have trained Americans to say anything anywhere, and because no longer does my editor see confession as intimate and full of silences, I happen to know so I tell her that Eli Lilly, the drug company that makes Prozac, is now marketing a new pill: PROZAC Weekly. Try to convince your doctor that taking a pill every day for depression is depressing, I suggest. We are all in this together, whenever, whatever, wherever—in detail is okay.

We are having lunch because I am writing a book on hepatotoxicity, also known as liver failure. In the public imagination, liver failure is associated with alcoholism, but the truth is 55 percent of the time liver failure is drug-induced. Again and again there exists an "I" who was institutionalized because "I swallowed a bottle of Tylenol and went into a coma. Now, I can say that luckily the coma did not lead to liver failure and death, but back then I was disappointed when I woke up in a hospital room. The waking was slow because of the drugs in my system. I remember being cold. I remember shaking. They wrapped me in blankets. There was a flat needle taped against my skin, piercing my arm. The nurse, in an effort to demonstrate how far I had come, informed me the day I was to check out that the first thing I'd asked when I first awoke was, Alive? She said she answered, Yes, love, you are alive. When she told me this story she smiled and two cavernous dimples appeared on either cheek. Why are you smiling? Why are you smiling, my smiling nurse?"

My editor asks me to tell her exactly what the liver means to me. She must not have read Laurie Tarkan's article in the *Times*, though she pulls it from her briefcase and places it in the middle of the table. I point to a paragraph and read aloud: *The liver is particularly vulnerable to drugs because one of its functions is to break down or metabolize chemicals that are not water-soluble. . . . But sometimes the breakdown products are toxic to liver cells. Indeed it is surprising, given the noxious chemicals that the liver is exposed to, that more drugs do not damage it.*

> I've read all that already.
> Oh.
> You haven't answered my question.

She starts to gather her things. I remain seated in the restaurant a full hour after she leaves. I understand that what she wants is an explanation of the mysterious connections that exist between an author and her text. If I am present in a subject position, what responsibility do I have to the content, to the truth value, of the words themselves? Is "I" even me or am "I" a gearshift to get from one sentence to the next? Should I say we? Is the voice not various if I take responsibility for it? What does my subject mean to me?

Why do I care about the liver? I could have told her it is because the word *live* hides within it. Or we might have been able to do something with the fact that the liver is the largest single internal organ next to the soul, which looms large though it is hidden.

In truth I know the answer to her question, but how can I say to her, *Understand without effort that man is left, at times thinking, as if trying to weep.* I am somewhat rephrasing the poet César Vallejo because Vallejo comes closest to explaining that any kind of knowledge can be a prescription against despair, but she wouldn't accept his answer, she couldn't really use it for ad copy.

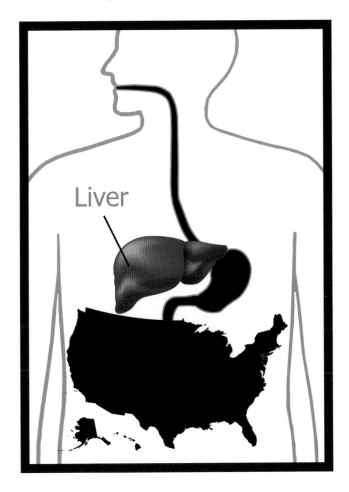

And I am not exactly a crying person, though my eyes tear up frequently because of my allergies. In any case, the other tears, the ones that express emotions, the ones that recognize and take responsibility for the soul don't come. Instead I get a sharp pain in my gut. And though heart disease is the leading killer of American women, the pain has nothing to do with that. I have had it all my life. Not quite a caving in, just a feeling of bits of my inside twisting away from flesh in the form of a blow to the body.

Sometimes I look into someone's face and I must brace myself—the blow on its way. For instance, I go into my bedroom to put on socks because my toes could be cold and on the TV is Abner Louima: *I hope what comes out of my case is change. What happened to me should not happen to any human being, to my children or anybody else's children . . .*

It's been four years since he was sodomized with a broken broomstick while in police custody. It was two months and three surgeries before he could leave the hospital. He has just agreed to a settlement with the city and the police union for 8.7 million dollars. Louima's lawyer, Johnny L. Cochran Jr., is standing next to him. Louima looks okay. A reporter asks him how it feels to be a rich man. Not rich, says Louima. Lucky, lucky to be alive. Instinctively my hand braces my abdomen.

And the other: All the shots, all forty-one never add up, never become plural, and will not stay in the past. It felt wasteful to cry at the television set as Amadou Diallo's death was announced.

Sometimes I think it is sentimental, or excessive, certainly not intellectual, or perhaps too naïve, too self-wounded to value each life like that, to feel loss to the point of being bent over each time. There is no innovating loss. It was never invented, it happened as something physical, something physically experienced. It is not something an "I" discusses socially. Though Myung Mi Kim did say that the poem is really a responsibility to everyone in a social space. She did say it was okay to cramp, to clog, to fold over at the gut, to have to put hand to flesh, to have to hold the pain, and then to translate it here. She did say, in so many words, that what alerts, alters.

I felt it too.

The loneliness?

I let it happen.

By feeling?

By not not feeling.

That's too much . . .

Like dying?

Maybe, or death is second.

Second to what?

To loneliness.

Define loneliness.

Why are we alive? My sister had a daughter and a son. Is she dead? Is he dead? Yes, they're dead. My sister's children and her husband died in a car crash. She is a psychiatrist, but she cannot help herself. She does not, probably cannot, legally, prescribe herself any drugs. Her world—she is letting it—is crumbling. "*Why* . . ." "*What* . . ."

I listen, but do not speak. I look into her eyes. We sit on the floor of public places, our faces wet. Then, like that, I am in my car, turning the key in the ignition, my own quotidian affairs breaking in. Who will she be when she is too tired to cry? Where does her kind of grief go? Paul Celan whispers in my ear,

> All those sleep shapes, crystalline
> that you assumed
> in the language shadow,
>
> to those
> I lead my blood,
>
> those image lines, them
> I'm to harbour
> in the slit-arteries
> of my cognition—,
>
> *my grief, I can see,*
> *is deserting you.*

Define loneliness?

Yes.

It's what we can't do for each other.

What do we mean to each other?

What does a life mean?

Why are we here if not for each other?

Or a friend's mother dies when she is on her way home from her father's funeral in Switzerland. While her plane crosses the Atlantic, her mother dies of a heart attack in New Hampshire. I run into this friend in SoHo at the Cupping Room. She is wearing a long fur coat.

It was my mother's. She died . . .

This woman, a college friend, seems fine. Perhaps we are not responsible for the lives of our parents—not in our pores or our very breath. We can expect. We can resolve. We can come to terms with. Afterwards we wear their clothing, sit in their chairs, and remember them. Profoundly remember them. But we are not responsible. The construct of my sister, this character, feels erased. Anything, I tell her. I write in my notes, I will do anything. In truth I can do nothing but see in the activity of her grief three people's death. The end of each day is followed by morning.

A husband wakes up beside me, stretching, asking,

Sweetheart, honey, dearest,
how did you sleep?

We hear on the television that a thirteen-year-old boy is convicted of first-degree murder for killing a six-year-old girl when he was twelve years old.

I, or we, it hardly matters, seek out the story in the *Times*. The girl had a torn liver, fractured skull, and broken ribs—perhaps there was more. In any case, her time is done. The boy was tried as an adult or he was tried as a dead child. There are no children anymore, at least not this boy—this boy who is only a child. But then, what child behaves like this? What child behaves like this, knows the consequences, and still insists he was playing at being a wrestler? To know and not to understand is perhaps one definition of being a child. Or responsibility is not connected to sense-making, the courts have decided.

In this moment we are alone with the facts as he will be when he understands. In the time it takes for the appeal to happen, he will be a dead child in an adult prison. He will be alive as someone else. He will be there with adults and because his life is happening in this way, he will forever happen in our minds as a dead child. I see the tears have run relatively parallel down his mother's cheeks. What I have is a headache. On the Tylenol bottle someone has made a distinction between adults and children. I, as an adult, am allowed two tablets. As I stare at the label, from somewhere a voice whispers in my ear: Take comfort in our strength.

In an attempt to convey a desired sense, a kind of bastardized *constructio ad sensum*, I claim the dream where I am sitting on a huge pill bottle.

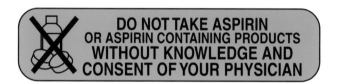

DO NOT TAKE ASPIRIN
OR ASPIRIN CONTAINING PRODUCTS
WITHOUT KNOWLEDGE AND
CONSENT OF YOUR PHYSICIAN

It is so tall I would have to jump to reach the ground. The white safety cap moves a little, but will not unscrew. I can see all the pills, perhaps placebos, stacked up inside even as I am sitting above them. The pills are reflected in a season of other overturned pill bottles. Because I am up so high I can't see anyone else, but I can hear the audio: She is dead, finished, no dreamscape can help her now.

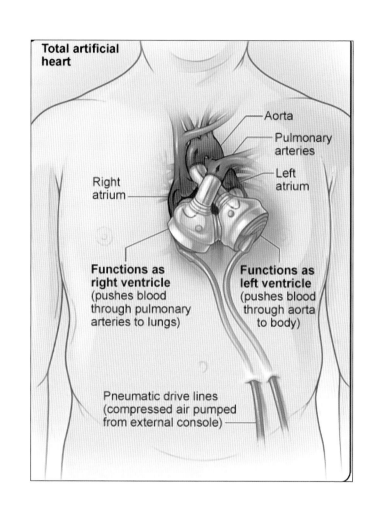

Total artificial heart

Aorta

Pulmonary arteries

Left atrium

Right atrium

Functions as right ventricle (pushes blood through pulmonary arteries to lungs)

Functions as left ventricle (pushes blood through aorta to body)

Pneumatic drive lines (compressed air pumped from external console)

Mr. Tools, for a while the only person in the world walking around with an artificial heart, said the weirdest thing was being without a heartbeat. His was a private and perhaps lonely singularity. No one else could say, I know how you feel. The only living being without a heartbeat, he had a whirr instead. It was not the same whirr of a siren, but rather the fast repetitive whirr of a machine whose insistent motion might eventually seem like silence.

Mr. Tools had the ultimate tool in his body. He felt its heaviness. The weight on his heart was his heart. All his apparatus—artificial heart, energy coil, battery, and controller—weighed more than four pounds. The whirr if you are not Mr. Tools is detectable only with a stethoscope. For Mr. Tools, that whirr was his sign that he was alive.

I realize that death is inevitable, but I also realize that if there's an opportunity to extend it, you take it.

Robert Tools

A friend drops by my home to visit, but I have at just that moment put on my coat. We leave and go to sit in Sal's Pizzeria at the corner. Our conversation drifts until she says, I didn't like Coetzee's *Disgrace*. I recommended this novel to her so I smile because I feel accused of some wrongdoing, but I am also amused because it really doesn't matter, does it? He's not for everyone, I say. There's always another book to read. I recommend Zadie Smith's *White Teeth*. This friend won't be shrugged off. She wants to know why so many intelligent people like *Disgrace*. I want to tell her that if she stopped thinking about people as intelligent she might know why. I say instead something about nobody learning anything from history and that South Africa's Truth and Reconciliation Commission is being critiqued perhaps. I don't know. I try again by claiming Coetzee is suggesting the land is what survives. In the end he is a naturalist. I don't know, I think this before I say it. I chew on my pizza and wonder what a naturalist is, what the word means beyond its obvious commitment to natural laws. Does it have anything to do with euthanasia? She sits across from me in silence, she doesn't respond, doesn't initiate. Did you know Petrus means rock? I ask. Petrus is the name of the major Black character in the novel. As if I hadn't spoken, she asks emphatically, what woman hasn't been raped? In the novel Petrus ignores a rape. I make no response. She goes to the bathroom. While she is in there, I put on my coat. After we part and I am climbing the stairs to my apartment, I think surely some percentage of women hasn't been raped. I don't know though, really. Perhaps this is the kind of thing I could find out on Google.

Q

Google Search   I'm Feeling Lucky

Then I think, maybe, that "what woman hasn't been raped" could be another way of saying "this is the most miserable in my life."

Or while on vacation in a village in the Caribbean, I feel ill and a doctor gives me medication with an expiration date that has long come and gone. I point this out to the nurse. She lifts the sheet of tablets from my outstretched palm while adjusting her glasses with her other hand. She knows she has asked me if I have any liver disease. And though these orally disintegrating tablets are in the FDA pregnancy category B, meaning they are not likely to harm an unborn baby, she has also remembered to ask if I am pregnant. I am not, nor am I nursing, which turns out to be fortuitous since it is not known if this drug will pass into breast milk. The only bothersome fact then is the expired expiration date. Well, the nurse says in a tone of voice that implies condemnation neither of the pills nor of the woman standing before her. I take back the tablets she holds out to me. After I leave the clinic, I sit in a bar bordering the sea and watch the waves come crashing in. I order a glass of lemon water and a drink called "Between the Sheets." Drying my hands, I peel back the foil backing of the blister and gently remove the first tablet. I do not try to push the tablet through the foil backing, as it may break. I then peel back the foil backing of another blister and gently remove that tablet. I immediately place the tablets on my tongue where they dissolve in seconds. I could swallow with saliva, but I take a drink of my water. I do not experience any uncommon but serious side effects. I have no allergic reaction; no difficulty breathing; no closing of my throat; no swelling of my lips, tongue, or face; no hives. Even after a few sips of my drink I experience no irregular heartbeats; no muscle cramps or uncontrollable movements. There is no need for me to seek emergency medical attention or contact the doctor. Eventually, without peeling back any more foil, I feel fine.

I ask my sister if she's seen the commercial for Diflucan, a new yeast-infection medication that is less messy than the suppository Monistat. One rare but possible side effect of Diflucan is liver damage. Monistat is to suppository inconvenience as Diflucan is to possible liver damage—What is wrong with this picture?

I'm amused, but my sister is distracted because she has been asked to assess the value of her dead children's lives. She has to meet with an insurance adjuster. So far they have only spoken on the phone. He wants her to put together information on her children, think of it as a scrapbook, he'd said. Report cards, medical records, extracurricular activities. My sister isn't crying as she tells me this. Instead she seems distracted and impatient. I am asking the questions she asked the adjuster and she is irritated with this reflection of herself. She wants to say to me the two words she wanted to say to him.

In preparation and by chance I read a piece about insurance adjusters in *Harper's* written by a guy named Adam Davidson. The title "Working Stiffs" had the flat humor of puns—ha ha humor. More than anything I want to tell my sister about Davidson's piece, but I don't want to risk generalizing her experience. What I know, I know because of Davidson; what she knows, she knows because she is being made to perform a life I don't want to live. I ask questions, all the ones Davidson has already answered.

Mostly we discuss what should and should not be included in the portrait of her children's lives. Mostly we agree. Each activity is a sign, a sign that points to social class, which points to potential worth. The private school, the tennis lessons, the soccer team, the scuba medal, the collection of exotic fish or lack thereof were all heading somewhere. It is not a destination we need to arrive at since clearly the children did not arrive there. Ultimately no one lives in that place. It is a place of compensation divorced from compassion. It is a reasonable place created by adults for adults after the fact of loss.

On the bus two women argue about whether Rudy Giuliani had to kneel before the Queen of England when he was knighted. One says she is sure he had to. They all had to, Sean Connery, John Gielgud, Mick Jagger. They all had to. The other one says that if he had, they would have seen it on television. We would have seen him do it. I am telling you we would have seen it happen.

When my stop arrives, I am still considering Giuliani as nobility. It is difficult to separate him out from the extremes connected to the city over the years of his mayorship. Still, a day after the attack on the World Trade Center a reporter asked him to estimate the number of dead. His reply—More than we can bear—caused me to turn and look at him as if for the first time. It is true that we carry the idea of us along with us. And then there are three thousand dead and it is incomprehensible and ungraspable. Physically and emotionally we cannot bear it, should in fact never have this capacity. So when the number is released, it is a sieve that cannot hold the loss Giuliani recognized and answered for.

Wallace Stevens wrote, "the peculiarity of the imagination is nobility . . . nobility which is our spiritual height and depth; and while I know how difficult it is to express it, nevertheless I am bound to give a sense of it. Nothing could be more evasive and inaccessible. Nothing distorts itself and seeks disguise more quickly. There is a shame of disclosing it and in its definite presentation a horror of it. But there it is."

Sir Giuliani kneeling. It was apparently not something to be seen on television, but rather a moment to be heard and experienced; a moment that allowed his imagination's encounter with death to kneel under the weight of the real.

Three days after the attack on the World Trade Center it rains. It rains through the night with a determination that peters off by morning. That same afternoon I go downtown to the site. The rain, I thought, would clear the air of smoke. It is still smoking because the debris is still burning. A rank smell is in the air. The rescue workers are there moving pieces of wreckage by hand. In the overcast, dim light they shadow the dead, are themselves deadened.

Their movements are so slow my eyes can rest in them. Something swallows the noise of the trucks. I see but do not hear them. The language of description competes with the dead in the air. My eyes burn and tear. Stacked up along the highway are the wooden stretchers that were never needed. Ink runs on the posters of the missing taped to the sides of buildings. The photographed faces are faded. In some places the rain cleared away the ash and the powdered concrete, in other places it matted the ash and concrete to window ledges, to car exteriors, to any and all available surfaces.

The policemen, their backs to the workers, stare at the public, the news people, everyone and anyone; each stands with his weight on one leg speaking under his breath to another. My sense is that whatever they are saying does not connect with the part of their brain that is there to police our curious grief.

Overnight Osama bin Laden becomes a household name. Laden, I am told, rhymes with sadden, not lawless. If I close my eyes, I can see him. He is of course being represented as Satan. He is a terrorist. His commitment to his interests extends beyond his need to be alive, perhaps beyond need or life itself.

In college, when I studied Hegel, I was struck by his explanation of the use of death by the state. Hegel argued that death is used as a threat to keep citizens in line. The minute you stop fearing death you are no longer controlled by governments and councils. In a sense you are no longer accountable to life. The relationships embedded between the "I" and the "we" unhinge and lose all sense of responsibility. That "you," functioning as other, now exists beyond our notions of civil and social space.

So terrorists embody that state of beyond; they are that freedom embodied. They bring that deathly state of lawlessness to life, or into life, and breathlessness to breath. They carry those whose lives they touch over into that dead, breathless realm. Sometimes they close the door behind them, but we can't forget it's there. Both states are strengthened by this knowledge. Antigone, the character not the play, by Theban definition was a domestic terrorist. Hegel uses her as an example. She identified with the dead, was willing to walk among them. In the course of the drama, even though she has many lines left to speak in the play, Creon describes her to her sister as already dead. So it is, was, already, with Osama's men.

Walking home I find myself singing softly to the tune of "Day-O," *Come Mister Taliban give us bin Laden.* This version of the song along with its accompanying animation was passed on to me via email and now I can't stop myself.

I am walking behind two big guys. One says to the other,

> I don't regret any part of my life. It's been a
> good life. Were anything to happen I could
> live with that.

I think he means he could live with his own death. I want to tell him he won't have to.

In a taxi speeding uptown on the West Side Highway, I let my thoughts drift below the surface of the Hudson until it finally occurs to me that feelings fill the gaps created by the indirectness of experience. Though the experience is social, thoughts carry it into a singular space and it is this that causes the feelings of loneliness; or it is this that collides the feeling with the experience so that what is left is the solitude called loneliness. And from that space of loneliness, I can feel the cab driver watching me in his rear-view mirror.

He wants to know if I attend Columbia University.

> Years ago, now I just live in the
> neighborhood.
>
> You seem like a smart lady. What do
> you do for your living?
>
> I write about the liver.
>
> The liver? Really? You are a doctor?
>
> No, no. I write about the liver
> because I'm thinking as if trying to weep.
>
> Excuse me? You think the liver
> is connected to thoughts?
>
> Well, not exactly.
>
> Anyway, tell me something, you have
> lived in this country many years?

Over thirty.

Well yes, then. So tell me this, have you
noticed these white people, they think
they are better than everyone else?

Have I noticed? Are you joking? You're
not joking. Where are you from?

Pakistan.

I see. It's only a few months since 9/11.
They think you're al Qaeda.

I know. But the things they say to me.
They don't know anything.

Be happy you can't read their thoughts, I want to say to
him. I smile into the rearview mirror instead. Why with
such a nice smile are you trying to weep? he asks as we
pull up to my building.

To roll over or not to roll over that IRA? To have a new iMac or not to have it? To eTrade or not to eTrade? Again and again these were Kodak moments, full of individuation; we were all on our way to our personal best. America was seemingly a meritocracy. I, I, I am Tiger Woods. It was the nineties. Now it is the twenty-first century and either you are with us or you are against us. Where is your flag?

It strikes me that what the attack on the World Trade Center stole from us is our willingness to be complex. Or what the attack on the World Trade Center revealed to us is that we were never complex. We might want to believe that we can condemn and we can love and we can condemn because we love our country, but that's too complex.

Over lunch, someone says,

> What's all this about detaining hundreds
> of people and monitoring lawyer-client
> conversations? Who do we think we are?
> China?

Inside the space of the constructed joke, everyone laughs
and laughs.

When New York City arrived home it received a message from the Postmaster General.

 UNITED STATES
POSTAL SERVICE.

What should make me suspect a piece of mail?

- It's unexpected or from someone you don't know.
- It's addressed to someone no longer at your address.
- It's handwritten and has no return address or bears one that you can't confirm is legitimate.
- It's lopsided or lumpy in appearance.
- It's sealed with excessive amounts of tape.
- It's marked with restrictive endorsements such as "Personal" or "Confidential."
- It has excessive postage.

What should I do with a suspicious piece of mail?

- Don't handle a letter or package that you suspect is contaminated.
- Don't shake it, bump it, or sniff it.
- Wash your hands thoroughly with soap and water.
- Notify local law enforcement authorities.

Two questions: What should make me suspect a piece of mail? What should I do with a suspicious piece of mail? These are apparently real questions. People are sick and have died. What should I do? I shouldn't shake it, bump it, or sniff it. I shouldn't handle it. I should notify authorities. I should wash my hands thoroughly with soap and water.

As the days pass I begin to watch myself closely. The America that I am is washing her hands. She is checking for a return address. She is noticing the postage amount. Then the moment comes: Inhalation anthrax or a common cold? I have to ask myself. Something happens—a new kind of white powder—and I am led inside. Do I like who I am becoming? Is this me? Fear. Fear in phlegm. Fear airborne. Fear foreign.

My flushing toilet, my hot water, my air conditioner, my health insurance, my, my, my—all my my's were American-made. This is how I was alive. Or I wasn't alive. I was a product, or I was like a product, a product of and like Walt Disney's cell animation—stylishly animated, somewhat comic. I used to think of myself as a fearless person.

Mahalia Jackson is a genius. Or Mahalia Jackson has genius. The man I am with is trying to make a distinction. I am uncomfortable with his need to make this distinction because his inquiry begins to approach subtle shades of racism, classism, or sexism. It is hard to know which. Mahalia Jackson never finished the eighth grade, or Mahalia's genius is based on the collision of her voice with her spirituality. True spirituality is its own force. I am not sure how to respond to all this.

We have just seen George Wein's documentary, *Louis Armstrong at Newport, 1971*. In the auditorium a room full of strangers listened to Mahalia Jackson sing "Let There Be Peace on Earth" and stood up and gave a standing ovation to a movie screen. Her clarity of vision crosses thirty years to address intimately each of us. It is as if her voice has always been dormant within us, waiting to be awakened, even though "it had to go through its own lack of answers, through terrifying silence, (and) through the thousand darknesses of murderous speech."

Perhaps Mahalia, like Paul Celan, has already lived all our lives for us. Perhaps that is the definition of genius. Hegel says, "Each man hopes and believes he is better than the world which is his, but the man who is better merely expresses this same world better than the others." Mahalia Jackson sings as if it is the last thing she intends to do. And even though the lyrics of the song are, "Let there be peace on earth and let it begin with me," I am hearing, *Let it begin in me*.

In my dream I apologize to everyone I meet. Instead of introducing myself, I apologize for not knowing why I am alive. I am sorry. I am sorry. I apologize. In real life, oddly enough, when I am fully awake and out and about, if I catch someone's eye, I quickly look away. Perhaps this too is a form of apology. Perhaps this is the form apologies take in real life. In real life the looking away is the apology, despite the fact that when I look away I almost always feel guilty; I do not feel as if I have apologized. Instead I feel as if I have created a reason to apologize, I feel the guilt of having ignored that thing—the encounter. I could have nodded, I could have smiled without showing my teeth. In some small way I could have wordlessly said, I see you seeing me and I apologize for not knowing why I am alive. I am sorry. I am sorry. I apologize. Afterwards, after I have looked away, I never feel as if I can say, Look, look at me again so that I can see you, so that I can acknowledge that I have seen you, so that I can see you and apologize.

A friend tells me this story: She goes to a bathhouse in Los Angeles and sees an old woman with an identification number on her arm. The markings begin with the letter A.

> I saw her concentration-camp number and that it started with the letter A. My cousin has the same one. So I said, "My cousin was in the same concentration camp as you. Auschwitz."

> I was in Auschwitz, but how did you know?

> Because of the A.

It turns out the A's collision with Auschwitz is pure coincidence. The A in the identification number stands for the German word for worker—*arbeiter*.

> You think the A stands for location, but it stands for function.

What my friend wanted to communicate to me about that conversation was that "Frieda Berger and I had defied history in order to have it. She was supposed to be dead, and I was supposed to have never been born. And we both lived, and found each other in LA, and she was able to tell me this detail about the letter A. A detail that allows me to begin to be true to her life as precisely as it is lived."

When I remember this story half a year later, it is because of its detail of correction. The fact that Ariel Sharon wishes to exile Yasser Arafat from Palestine immediately pulls this mis-equation from my memory.

> You think the A stands for location, but it
> stands for function.

Sharon's desire to exile Arafat allows me to feel tender toward Sharon. I think of him waking in the middle of the night, after he has slept enough to feel almost awake. I think of him waking into this thought, a thought that strips the Israeli/Palestinian conflict of all its complexities. Simply separate Arafat from his people. I see him forgetting that Arafat is already exiled, that he himself in the eyes of some is also in a state of exile. Sharon's solution is so simple it makes me want to touch his face.

Arafat exiled. It is not a reasonable wish. Eventually Colin Powell will tell Sharon this. Arafat is the legitimate, recognized leader of the Palestinians. He is also not every Palestinian who believes in his right of return. He is not every person who still holds on his person the keys to his former home. Arafat is not the leader of Hamas. But at some hour, for Sharon, the security of Israel rests within a body and its location. At some hour Sharon feels the desperation of displacement as devastation, an impotence. He works it out, and at some hour Arafat's location as alien, as exile, is to be Sharon's greatest contribution to the road map to peace in the Middle East, greater than any function he presently serves.

The Sunday I turn forty the delivery guy pulls the front door shut as I pick up the phone to call my parents and thank them for the lilies. "A lovely flower. I carried them on my (birth) day and now I place them in this vase in memory of something that has died," Katharine Hepburn in *Stage Door*. My parents' housekeeper answers the phone.

May I speak to my mother?

They're still at the funeral.

Whose funeral?

Is everyone you know alive?

It occurs to me that forty could be half my life or it could be all my life. On the television I am told I don't want to look like I am forty. Forty means I might have seen something hard, something unpleasant, or something dead. I might have seen it and lived beyond it in time. Or I might have squinted my eyes too many times in order to see it, I might have turned my face to the sun in order to look away. I might have actually been alive. With injections of Botox, short for botulism toxin, it seems I can see or be seen without being seen; I can age without aging. I have the option of worrying without looking like I worry. Each day of this life I could bite or shake doubt as if to injure or kill without looking as if anything mattered to me. I could paralyze facial muscles that cause wrinkles. All those worry and frown lines would disappear. I could purchase paralysis. I could choose that. Eventually the paralysis would sink in, become a deepening personality that need not, like Enron's "distorting factors," distort my appearance. I could be all that seems, or rather I could be all that I am—fictional. Ultimately I could face reality undisturbed by my own mortality.

At the airport-security checkpoint on my way to visit my grandmother, I am asked to drink from my water bottle.

This water bottle?

That's right. Open it and drink from it.

At the airport-security checkpoint on my way to visit my grandmother, I am asked to take off my shoes.

Take off my shoes?

Yes. Both please.

At the airport-security checkpoint on my way to visit my grandmother, I am asked if I have a fever.

A fever? Really?

Yes. Really.

My grandmother is in a nursing home. It's not bad. It doesn't smell like pee. It doesn't smell like anything. When I go to see her, as I walk through the hall past the common room and the nurses' station, old person after old person puts out his or her hand to me. Steven, one says. Ann, another calls. It's like being in a developing country, but instead of food or money you are what is wanted, your company. In developing countries I have felt overwhelmingly American, calcium-rich, and privileged. Here, I feel young, lucky, and sad. Sad is one of those words that has given up its life for our country, it's been a martyr for the American dream, it's been neutralized, co-opted by our culture to suggest a tinge of discomfort that lasts the time it takes for this and then for that to happen, the time it takes to change a channel. But sadness is real because once it meant something real. It meant dignified, grave; it meant trustworthy; it meant exceptionally bad, deplorable, shameful; it meant massive, weighty, forming a compact body; it meant falling heavily; and it meant of a color: dark. It meant dark in color, to darken. It meant me. I felt sad.

My grandmother tells me that since the doctor told her to stay away from cigarettes she now smokes the longest ones she can find. Actually she continues to smoke a pack of Marlboros a day. I tell her Philip Morris is changing their name to Altria. From behind a screen of smoke my grandmother says, We should all change our names when we don't like what we see in the mirror. It's an easy way to distance the self from the self, I say for the conversation's sake. She and I sit outside in the sun during the dead of winter smoking cigarettes, chewing gum, and watching the cars go by. Sitting here, chewing Juicy Fruit until the taste evaporates, makes me think of the last line of that movie *Secrets and Lies*: "This is the life."

I don't usually talk to strangers, but it is four o'clock and I can't get a cab. I need a cab because I have packages, but it's four o'clock and all the cabs are off duty. They are making a shift change. At the bus stop I say, It's hard to get a cab now. The woman standing next to me glances over without turning her head. She faces the street where cab after cab drives by with its light off. She says, as if to anyone, It's hard to live now. I don't respond. Hers is an Operation Iraqi Freedom answer. The war is on and the Department of Homeland Security has decided we have an elevated national-threat level, a code-orange alert. I could say something, but my packages are getting heavier by the minute and besides, what is there to say since rhetorically it's not about our oil under their sand but about freeing Iraqis from Iraqis and Osama is Saddam and Saddam is "that man who tried to kill my father" and the weapons of mass destruction are, well, invisible and Afghanistan is Iraq and Iraq is Iran and we see ourselves only through our own eyes and the British, but not the French, and Germany won't and Turkey won't join us but the coalition is inside Baghdad where the future is the threat the Americans feel they can escape though there is no escaping the Americans because war, this war, is about peace: "The war in Iraq is really about peace. Trying to make the world more peaceful. This victory in Iraq, when it happens, will make the world more peaceful."

In the elevator the yellow ribbon tied to the flowerpot in the front of the building is under discussion. Nick, the super, tied a yellow ribbon but didn't do the flag thing. This distinction is not lost on anyone. The lawyer in 5B says the super should be careful he doesn't lose his job. My left eyebrow lifts, but the lawyer does not notice, he does not see it, he does not receive it legally.

"Certain absences are so stressed, so ornate, so planned, they call attention to themselves; arrest us with intentionality and purpose. . . . Where . . . is the shadow of the presence from which the text has fled?"

Toni Morrison

THE PHARMACEUTICAL MANUFACTURERS' ASSOCIATION OF SOUTH AFRICA

ALCON LABORATORIES (S.A.) (PROPRIETARY) LIMITED

BAYER (PROPRIETARY) LIMITED

BRISTOL-MYERS SQUIBB (PROPRIETARY) LIMITED

BYK MADAUS (PROPRIETARY) LIMITED

ELI LILLY (SOUTH AFRICA) (PROPRIETARY) LIMITED

GLAXO WELLCOME (SOUTH AFRICA) (PROPRIETARY) LIMITED

HOECHST MARION ROUSSEL LIMITED

INGELHEIM PHARMACEUTICALS (PROPRIETARY) LIMITED

JANSSEN-CILAG PHARMACEUTICA (PROPRIETARY) LIMITED

KNOLL PHARMACEUTICALS SOUTH AFRICA (PROPRIETARY) LIMITED

LUNDBECK SOUTH AFRICA (PROPRIETARY) LIMITED

MERCK (PROPRIETARY) LIMITED

MSD (PROPRIETARY) LIMITED

NOVARTIS SOUTH AFRICA (PROPRIETARY) LIMITED

NOVO NORDISK (PROPRIETARY)
LIMITED

PHARMACIA & UPJOHN
(PROPRIETARY) LIMITED

RHONE-POULENC RORER SOUTH
AFRICA (PROPRIETARY) LIMITED

ROCHE PRODUCTS
(PROPRIETARY) LIMITED

SCHERING (PROPRIETARY) LIMITED

SCHERING-PLOUGH
(PROPRIETARY) LIMITED

S.A. SCIENTIFIC PHARMACEUTICALS
(PROPRIETARY) LIMITED

SMITHKLINE BEECHAM PHARMACEUTICALS
(PROPRIETARY) LIMITED

UNIVERSAL PHARMACEUTICALS
(PROPRIETARY) LIMITED

WYETH (PROPRIETARY) LIMITED

XIXIA PHARMACEUTICALS
(PROPRIETARY) LIMITED

ZENECA SOUTH AFRICA
(PROPRIETARY) LIMITED

BAYER AG

BOEHRINGER-INGELHEIM
INTERNATIONAL GmbH

BOEHRINGER-INGELHEIM KG

BRISTOL-MYERS SQUIBB COMPANY

BYK GULDEN LOMBERG
CHEMISCHE FABRIK GmbH

ELI LILLY AND COMPANY

Or over breakfast the *New York Times* is barely visible beneath the boxes of cereal, juice, and milk, but because I have been waiting for this day without realizing I was waiting, I see the story at first glance: President Mbeki has decided antiretrovirals will be made available to the five million South Africans infected by the HIV virus.

My body relaxes. My shoulders fall back. I had not known that my distress at Mbeki's previous position against distribution of the drugs had physically lodged itself like a virus within me.

Before Mbeki, thirty-nine drug companies filed suit in order to prevent South Africa's manufacture of generic AIDS drugs. Possible trade sanctions were threatened. Then President Clinton did an about-face and the lawsuit was dismissed. But like an absurdist dream, Mbeki stood between the now available drugs and the dying.

It is not possible to communicate how useless, how much like a skin-sack of uselessness I felt. *I am better than thou art now: I am a fool, the fool said, thou art nothing.* Is she dead? Is he dead? Yes, they are dead. One observes, one recognizes without being recognized. One opens the paper. One turns on the television. Nothing changes. My distress grows into nothing. Thou art nothing.

Such distress moved in with muscle and bone. Its entrance by necessity slowly translated my already grief into a tremendously exhausted hope. The translation occurred unconsciously, perhaps occurred simply because I am alive. The translation occurs as a form of life. Then life, which seems so full of waiting, awakes suddenly into a life of hope.

Life is a form of hope?

If you are hopeful.

Maybe hope is the same as breath—part of what it means to be human and alive.

Or maybe hoping is the same as waiting. It can be futile.

Waiting for what?

For a life to begin.

I am here.

And I am still lonely.

Then all life is a form of waiting, but it is the waiting of loneliness. One waits to recognize the other, to see the other as one sees the self. Levinas writes, "The subject who speaks is situated in relation to the other. This privilege of the other ceases to be incomprehensible once we admit that the first fact of existence is neither being in itself nor being for itself but being for the other, in other words, that human existence is a creature. By offering a word, the subject putting himself forward lays himself open and, in a sense, prays."

When she comes toward me I stiffen. But it's all right. It's nothing. The pamphlet says in bold letters, **BE LIKE JESUS**. Because I was brought up this way, I wait two blocks before tossing it. Be your own Christ. I'll remember that or I remember that. As if it were a soul memory, I say aloud to Neo, be like Jesus. I am on my way home from seeing *The Matrix Reloaded*. The film's superhero, Neo, can't save anyone; Morpheus will have to have another dream: the one in which salvation narratives are passé; the one in which people live no matter what you dream; the one in which people die no matter what you dream; or no matter what, you dream—

Because the foundations for loneliness begin in the dreamscapes you create. Their resemblance to reality reflects disappointment first.

Then my father dies and I cannot attend the funeral. It is not possible. I telephone my mother. We speak daily. I recommend cremation. I defend my recommendation. I send flowers. What I want to send is a replacement mourner. It seems odd that I can neither rent nor buy this; no grieving service is available. I mention this to a friend. She says that at her father's funeral in China they hired many mourners—the more mourners, the better. Many, many mourners show many, many dollars, she explains.

At night I dream about my replacement mourner, a woman. She has lost her mother years before and because she is already grieving she just continues attending funerals for a price. Like a wet nurse, the prerequisite is a state of "already grief." Still, all the narrative control in the world does not offer me insight into her occupation. One creates her motivations and her tears, but cannot understand why she stays by the corpse—"with him" is the phrase no one utters, especially not with him "gone." Or one looks into the mourner's face and wants life to matter more. In the dream we talk about what a lonely occupation she has chosen. No, she says, you, you are the one with the lonely occupation. Death follows you into your dreams. The loneliness in death is second to the loneliness of life.

She's dying? From somewhere my sister, this character, hears this. Is she dead? She wakes to find herself wet; her nightgown wet, her face wet. Night sweats. In the day she understands. The pills say this is a possible side effect. They say in order to block pain sensations from being sent to the brain other things can happen. Nocturnal hyperhydrosis or night sweats happen. She calls me. No hello.

Night sweats.

Oh, the Zoloft?

At 2:47 a.m. she wakes beneath the wet sheet and decides to take a cold shower. On her way to the bathroom she turns on the television.

"Ladies and Gentlemen, we got him." Saddam Hussein has been discovered in a hole in the ground. Someone with latex gloves has a tongue depressor in Hussein's mouth. The inside of his mouth looks very red. She pauses because this is meant to be important. It is supposed to mean something about peace. The newscaster, speaking very quickly, hopes this will be the end of the killings in Iraq. He says something else about the tongue depressor, but the shower drowns him out.

She closes her eyes against the water beating down. Would the natural coldness of the earth prevent night sweats? she wonders. Would a spider hole be considered a homeopathic cure for feeling like a corpse?

I would have to drink five more cups of coffee a day to reduce my chances of getting type 2 diabetes. I usually have one cup in the morning. Today I am staring into a possible second cup, and I do not see my husband's expression when I tell him about the darkness and the curtain.

I have a dream, or rather, in my dream the lights are out in New York City. They are out because they were out. Even inside the dream I know I am dreaming. The events of my dream are a form of mimesis. The darkness that accompanied the blackout existed, but does not now in the world outside the dream. In my dream the lights are out because I cannot see ahead of me. Or in this dark dream I am looking for a chance, "my chance to" or "my chance for"—it is not clear. Then where I am going or what I want is behind a black curtain, but it is so dark the curtain becomes the night. I want to fall asleep inside my dream. This wish for further paralysis wakes me.

You think voting won't make a difference, says my husband. This might be a wise thing to think. He says all this without lifting his gaze from the morning paper.

My dream is about a voting booth? I am not convinced. He is not interested in convincing me. He is reading about the candidates for the presidency. He is wondering if voting against someone is enough motivation to drag a country away from its inevitable course. Sometimes you read something and a thought that was floating around in your veins organizes itself into the sentence that reflects it. This might also be a form of dreaming.

Or I remember that the last two sentences I read in Fanny Howe's *Tis of Thee* before falling asleep the previous night were: "I learned to renounce a sense of independence by degrees and finally felt defeated by the times I lived in. Obedient to them."

Or, well, I tried to fit language into the shape of usefulness. The world moves through words as if the bodies the words reflect did not exist. The world, like a giant liver, receives everyone and everything, including these words: Is he dead? Is she dead? The words remain an inscription on the surface of my loneliness. This loneliness stems from a feeling of uselessness. Then Coetzee's Costello says in her fictional lecture, "for instants at a time I know what it is like to be a corpse."

Or "Your truly lonely Paul Celan" said that the poem was no different from a handshake. *I cannot see any basic difference between a handshake and a poem*—is how Rosmarie Waldrop translated his German. The handshake is our decided ritual of both asserting (I am here) and handing over (here) a self to another. Hence the poem is that—Here. I am here. This conflation of the solidity of presence with the offering of this same presence perhaps has everything to do with being alive.

Or one meaning of here is "In this world, in this life, on earth. In this place or position, indicating the presence of," or in other words, I am here. It also means to hand something to somebody—Here you are. Here, he said to her. Here both recognizes and demands recognition. I see you, or here, he said to her. In order for something to be handed over a hand must extend and a hand must receive. We must both be here in this world in this life in this place indicating the presence of.

Notes

Page 5

Researchers at Arizona State University conducted a study of violence in the top-5-grossing movies from 1964, 1974, 1984, and 1994 to determine trends in on-screen violence over time. The number of deaths had, in fact, increased from an average of 8 to 15 deaths per film. Notably, the 41 deaths found in the films from 1964 were nongraphic in nature, while 62% of deaths in the movies from 1994 were depicted graphically.

Shipley, Wes & Gray, Cavender. 2001. "Murder and Mayhem at the Movies." *Journal of Criminal Justice and Popular Culture* 9(1): pp. 1–14.

Page 7

1–800–SUICIDE is the phone number for the National Hopeline Network. It is an organization that links together crisis-prevention hotlines located locally throughout the United States. The network's purpose is to provide an easy-to-remember, toll-free phone number for people contemplating suicide. All member groups are certified by the American Association of Suicidology. In 2022, 988 became the Suicide & Crisis Lifeline.

See Lyn Hejinian's *Happily* (California: The Post-Apollo Press, 2000).

happily (not to be confused with *haply—adv.* [Archaic] by chance or accident; perhaps)—*adv.* form of HAPPY

happiness—n. form of HAPPY

happy—adj. 1 favored by circumstances; lucky; fortunate. *2* having, showing, or causing a feeling of great pleasure, contentment, joy, etc.; joyous; glad; pleased. *3* exactly appropriate to the occasion; suitable and clever; apt; felicitous [a *happy* suggestion]. *4* intoxicated, or irresponsibly quick to act, as if intoxicated: sometimes used in hyphenated compounds: see SLAP-HAPPY, TRIGGER-HAPPY.

"happy." *Webster's New World College Dictionary: Fourth Edition* (Foster City: IDG Books Worldwide, 2000), p. 647.

"haply." *Webster's New World College Dictionary: Fourth Edition* (Foster City: IDG Books Worldwide, 2000), p. 646.

Page 8

If breast cancer is missed on one year's mammogram, a woman's life expectancy is not usually altered, offering her little recourse under the law. However, the necessary treatments required are considerably more intense, causing remarkable physical, emotional, and financial difficulties.

Page 9

Retired nurse Frances Pollack of Hampshire, England, at the age of 85 paid £25 for a "Do Not Resuscitate" tattoo to be placed on her chest. She said this was in response to the frequency with which DNR wishes are not honored or not properly expressed to those resuscitating. "I don't want to die twice," Pollack said.

"Pensioner's 'Do Not Resuscitate' Tattoo." *BBC News World Edition*. http://news.bbc.co.uk/2/hi/health/2819149.stm (March 5, 2003).

Page 10

Both *Boogie Nights* (1997) and *Magnolia* (1999) were written and directed by Paul Thomas "P. T." Anderson. His first 2 major films received increasingly positive critical praise, but both failed at the box office. *Magnolia* was a particular commercial disappointment. In response, the 30-year-old Anderson made the unlikely decision of signing on as a writer for *Saturday Night Live* in 2000, to improve his comic-writing abilities.

P. T. Anderson's father, Ernie, was a voice actor, who raised his son in Studio City, California. Studio City is in the San Fernando Valley, the thriving center of the porn industry in the 1970s.

Tom Cruise was nominated for an Academy Award for Best Supporting Actor and won the Golden Globe Award in the same category for his role as Frank "T. J." Mackey in *Magnolia.*

Jason Robards, who played Earl Partridge, the father of Tom Cruise's character, died of cancer the year after *Magnolia* was released.

Page 11

Stein, Gertrude. *Wars I Have Seen* (New York: Random House, 1945), pp. 23–24.

Malcolm, Janet. "Gertrude Stein's War" in the *New Yorker* (June 2, 2003).

Page 15

In New York State, a "juvenile offender" is a child whose trial has gone through the adult court system, as opposed to a "juvenile delinquent," who has gone through the juvenile court system.

Page 17

Dementia in people under the age of 65 (presenile Alzheimer's) is not common. There are about 150 cases reported for every half million people.

Royal College of Psychiatrists, London. January, 2002. "Services for younger people with Alzheimer's and other Dementias—Council Report CR77": pp. 5–6.

HRC Manor Care was the second-largest owner and operator of long-term care centers in the United States. It operated more than 500 centers across the nation under names including Heartland, ManorCare, Arden Courts, and Springhouse. HCR ManorCare filed for bankruptcy in March 2018; a report by the *Washington Post* said that for the 5 years preceding the bankruptcy, the company had "exposed its roughly 25,000 patients to increasing health risks, according to inspection records." In July 2018, HCR ManorCare was acquired by nonprofit health system ProMedica. In 2020, ProMedica announced that it would begin to phase out the ManorCare name in favor of the new "ProMedica Senior Care" brand.

Spanko, Alex. "ProMedica to Phase Out HCR ManorCare Name, Rebrand Nursing Home Giant as ProMedica Senior Care." Skilled Nursing News, October 2, 2020, https://skillednursingnews.com/2020 /10/promedica-to-phase-out-hcr-manorcare-name-rebrand-nursing -home-giant-as-promedica-senior-care/. Accessed August 28, 2023.

Whoriskey, Peter and Dan Keating. "Overdoses, bedsores, broken bones: What happened when a private-equity firm sought to care for society's most vulnerable." *Washington Post*, November 25, 2018. https://www.washingtonpost.com/business/economy/opioid-overdoses -bedsores-and-broken-bones-what-happened-when-a-private-equity -firm-sought-profits-in-caring-for-societys-most-vulnerable/2018 /11/25/09089a4a-ed14-11e8-baac-2a674e91502b_story.html. Accessed August 28, 2023.

Brodsky, Joseph. "Song" in *Collected Poems in English* (New York: Farrar, Straus and Giroux, 2000), pp. 347–348.

Joseph Brodsky, the 1987 Nobel Prize–winner for Literature, and poet laureate of the United States during the presidency of George H. W. Bush, was born in the Soviet Union and exiled from his country at the age of 32. He made homes in Brooklyn, New York, and Massachusetts. It was in his apartment in Brooklyn that he died of a heart attack in 1996.

Page 18

Angela Lansbury starred as Jessica Fletcher for 12 seasons (1984–1996) in the hour-long murder-mystery drama *Murder, She Wrote*. In the nineties, she was also the program's producer. In the show, Fletcher is a successful mystery novelist, and former substitute teacher, from the fictional town of Cabot Cove. Traveling the country to promote her books, she repeatedly becomes an ad hoc murder investigator, due to the uncanny coincidence of death following her wherever she goes. Lansbury came to television after a successful 40-year feature-film career.

Page 21

Cornel West makes this point in his essay "Black Strivings in a Twilight Civilization," which is found in the collection of his and Henry Louis Gates Jr.'s essays, *The Future of the Race* (New York: Vintage Books, 1997).

optimism—n. 1 Philos. The doctrine held by Leibniz and others that the existing world is the best possible. *2* the tendency to take the most *hopeful* or cheerful view of matters or to expect the best outcome.
"optimism." *Webster's New World College Dictionary: Fourth Edition* (Foster City: IDG Books Worldwide, 2000), p. 1013.

On December 12, 2000, Vice President Al Gore conceded the presidential election to George W. Bush, bringing an end to the election dispute that began on November 7 of that year. Gore said he wished to "heal the divisions" created by the disputed outcomes.

On June 7, 1998, 3 men, John King, Lawrence Brewer, and Shawn Berry, offered James Byrd Jr. a ride home in Berry's pickup truck. Byrd was walking along a road in Jasper, a rural town in East Texas. He was returning home from his niece's bridal shower. Instead of bringing him home, the men brought him to a clearing in the woods where they beat him and chained him to the back of the truck. They then sped along a road just east of the town. Byrd's shredded torso was found first, and then his head, neck, and right arm were found about a mile away. Police said a trail of blood, body parts, and personal effects stretched for 2 miles. All 3 killers were found guilty of capital murder; Brewer and King were executed in 2011 and 2019, respectively, while Berry was given a life sentence with eligibility for parole beginning in 2038. In 2001, Texas lawmakers passed the James Byrd Jr. Hate Crimes Act; in 2009, President Obama signed the Matthew Shepard and James Byrd Jr. Hate Crimes Prevention Act into law. On the 25th anniversary of Byrd's death, in 2023, Jasper, Texas, passed a resolution proclaiming June 7 to be "James Byrd Jr. Day."

Page 23

Emily Dickinson's "Hope Is the Thing with Feathers" (using the traditional practice of titling her poems according to their first lines) was published as poem XXXII in the "Life" section of *The Complete Poems of Emily Dickinson*, first published by Little, Brown and Company in 1924. The version quoted below is from *The Poems of Emily Dickinson*, edited by R. W. Franklin and published by the Belknap Press of Harvard University Press, copyright 1998.

> "Hope" is the thing with feathers –
> That perches in the soul –
> And sings the tune without the words –
> And never stops – at all –
>
> And sweetest – in the Gale – is heard –
> And sore must be the storm –
> That could abash the little Bird
> That kept so many warm –
>
> I've heard it in the chillest land –
> And on the strangest Sea –
> Yet, never, in Extremity,
> It asked a crumb – of Me.

Cornel West discusses this issue in his essay "Nihilism in Black America," which is found in his book *Race Matters* (New York: Vintage Books, 1994).

Page 24

HBO did have a comedy series called *Not Necessarily the News* from 1983 to 1985 (the show was also revived for a brief and failed season in 1990). *NNTN* was a spoof of television news and took particular aim at political targets. The show is best remembered for Rich Hall's

"Sniglets" segment in which he proposed words that are not in the dictionary but should be, such as "Fictate (fik' tayt): v. To inform a television or screen character of impending danger under the assumption they can hear you," or "Noflet (nahf' lit): n. The upward swirl of hair found on certain individuals such as Ronald Reagan."

In late 2004, *The Sopranos* cast and production team began filming the sixth and final season of the critically and popularly acclaimed show. Once those 10 episodes were shown, viewing audiences were without new episodes of the show for the first time since 1998. In 2005, once all 86 total episodes had aired, HBO and A&E reached a syndication deal for a record-setting $200 million.

Between 1960 and 1975, over 600 Westerns were made, financed by European production companies. As the fifties came to an end, the American market no longer demanded the Western as it once did, and many European companies, particularly Italian ones, seized upon the opportunity to carry on the genre, which was still in great demand on their own continent. *The Good, the Bad, and the Ugly* (1966) is considered the quintessential spaghetti Western.

According to the Institute for Stress Management, our need for sleep decreases with age. Intuitively, we understand that babies need more sleep. Newborns get about 17 hours of sleep a day, while our need evens out at about 7 to 8 hours a night during puberty. This rate maintains for years, but the average adult's requirement for sleep begins to decrease again around 60 years of age, to about 6 hours.

Page 25

At the time of its release in 1969, audiences understood *The Wild Bunch* for its contemporary political implications. Its ample bloodshed portrayed a violence of tragedy, not romance, reflecting the realities of the Vietnam War. This boldness caused criticism of the film to be split, either enthusiastically lauding it or condemning it. In retrospect, it is almost universally considered one of the greatest Westerns ever made, both because of its novel approach to the genre and because of its historical significance as the direct precursor to a glut of lesser spaghetti Westerns.

Sam Peckinpah's own career almost died with something less of a flourish when he was fired from his gopher job on Liberace's television program for refusing to wear a suit. This allowed him to take a job as an assistant to Don Siegel, where he learned to direct films and made the connections to direct features himself. Known for his obstreperousness, perfectionism, and alcoholism (which was eventually partnered with rampant cocaine use), Peckinpah's whole career was a battle to remain a contributing member of the Hollywood community.

The image on this page does not depict a scene from the movie.

Page 29

Several sleep studies have noted that most people (both children and adults) who have trouble sleeping also have televisions in their rooms. Experts theorize that more often than not, the person gets involved in the program he or she is watching and stays up until the end.

In 2002, sales of the antidepressant Paxil were supported by an intense television-ad campaign that helped create $3.4 billion in sales, in the United States alone.[a] GlaxoSmithKline, the company that manufactures Paxil, had to radically adjust its marketing plans for the drug on August 19 of that year, when a federal court judge ruled that the corporation must stop showing any television commercial that did not make it clear that Paxil may be habit forming.[b]

[a] *Reuters News Service* (6/16/2003)
[b] *USA Today* (8/20/2002)

Julius Caesar is attributed with what is probably the most quoted example of parataxis: "Veni, vidi, vici"—"I came, I saw, I conquered."

Afterimages are a result of a desensitized retina that has been exposed to intense light for a prolonged period. The retina is the lining on the back of the eye and light produces chemical changes on it.

When you close your eyes, the desensitized part of the retina cannot respond as well to the change, creating an afterimage. Afterimages can sometimes last for 30 seconds or more.

Page 31

To deal with insomnia, physicians are increasingly prescribing drugs intended for other purposes, such as antidepressants. There is no compelling evidence that shows antidepressants improve sleep, according to Vaughn McCall, MD, an associate professor of psychiatry and behavioral medicine at Wake Forest University School of Medicine in Winston-Salem, North Carolina. He also said that antidepressants do not have a lower potential for adverse side effects than true hypnotics, drugs created for the purpose of promoting sleep.

"Pseudohypnotic Use Rises Despite Lack of Evidence on Efficacy." *Psychiatric News*. (July 7, 2000).

Page 32

The unnecessary use of medication, including sharing of medication, is referred to as "polypharmacy." The elderly are the most likely demographic group to engage in polypharmacy, with studies estimating that as many as 58% of the geriatric population takes part in the practice.

Page 35

There is a good chance that Czeslaw Milosz spent some time on the roofs of New York buildings in the late 1940s when he lived there as a diplomat for the Polish communist government.

"Gift" by Czeslaw Milosz ("Dar" in the original Polish) from *The Collected Poems* (New York: Ecco, 1988), p. 251.

Page 36

According to the New York State Department of Health, Bureau of Injury Prevention in 2004, a mean average of 175 suicides were reported in the borough of Manhattan each year (616 in the city as a whole). Additionally, at the time, an average of 797 people were hospitalized in Manhattan each year due to self-inflicted injury (3,552 throughout the five boroughs). Statistics for the causes of these self-inflicted injuries in females in New York State show that less than 1% could have been due to jumping off a building (fractures, central nervous system damage, etc.), as opposed to far more popular causes such as drug/medicinal poisoning (73.6%). Of all injuries attributed to falling in New York State, the most common single place of occurrence, by a large margin, is the home, with almost 40% of falls occurring there.

Page 39

The Museum of Emotions opened on Valentine's Day of 2000, funded by The Body Shop. The space showcases interactive art. It was part of a series of temporary "Museums of" set up on London's South Bank. It was directly preceded by the Museum of Me, and followed by the Museum of the Unknown.

Princess Diana died due to a car crash following a high-speed chase by the paparazzi through the streets of Paris. She was reported dead, as a result of cardiac arrest, at 4 a.m. on the morning of August 31, 1997.

On record, Diana Frances Spencer was born July 1, 1961. Her father was Lord Althrop, who later became Earl Spencer. Popularly, her death is questioned more than her birth. Many claim that it was faked as a way to more permanently shake media interest in her private affairs. Evidence cited includes the fact that her bodyguard seems to have impossibly survived the crash, and that very evening she told reporter Richard Kray that she soon planned to retire from public life.

Page 42

The 1982 film *Fitzcarraldo*, directed by Werner Herzog and starring Klaus Kinski, follows the story of an impresario who hopes to build an opera house in the deepest jungles of South America.

In the Irish system of nomenclature, the prefix "Fitz" means "bastard son of."

Werner Herzog is one of the leading directors of the New German Cinema movement. He is also a respected documentarian and even the subject of a documentary himself, *Werner Herzog Eats His Shoe* (the result of a bet in which he claimed that then film student, Errol Morris, would never complete a film). His collaborations with Kinski, a notably difficult actor, as Herzog himself is a notably demanding director, are infamous, and the subject of his film *My Best Fiend*.

Movie Place, a video rental store located near West 105th Street and Broadway, stocked up to 24,000 titles—compared to the average rental franchise's 5,000. It closed in 2006.

Page 43

Lithium was approved by the FDA in 1970 as a treatment for bipolar affective disorder ("manic depressive illness"). Its dosing varies widely, and often must be adjusted on a weekly basis. Prescribing of lithium decreased from 1996 to 2015 and, according to a 2020 report in the *Journal of Affective Disorders*, "has remained stable since."

Yian Lin et al. "Trends in prescriptions of lithium and other medications for patients with bipolar disorder in office-based practices in the United States: 1996–2015." *Journal of Affective Disorders* vol. 276 (2020): 883-889, https://doi.org/10.1016/j.jad.2020.07.063.

The character Fitzcarraldo was certainly inspired by the film's director himself. One of the movie's highlights is a scene in which the native South Americans pull a more than 300-ton steamship over a mountain. There are no special effects used in this scene; Herzog actually had his crew pull a steamship over a mountain. Rumors still persist of local movie technicians plotting their revenge on Herzog.

Page 47

Timothy McVeigh was put to death by lethal injection on Monday, June 11, 2001. He was the first federal prisoner put to death in 38 years. On March 15, 1963, Victor Feguer was hanged at the Iowa State

Penitentiary at Fort Madison, found guilty of kidnapping Dr. Edward Bartel and taking him across state lines to kill him.

On April 19, 1995, when McVeigh set off a truck bomb outside the Alfred P. Murrah Federal Building in Oklahoma City, he committed what is considered the worst act of domestic (homegrown) terrorism in US history, with its death toll of 168. A new Oklahoma City federal building opened in December of 2003. The new building with its floor-to-ceiling steel-plated main entrance, shatterproof glass, and waist-high concrete plugs, cost $33 million.

McVeigh's clean-shaven, close-cropped appearance seems to be representative of his early biography. He was a decorated infantryman (a tank gunner) in the first Gulf War, earning 4 medals of honor, including the Army Commendation Medal. He then tried out for the Army's elite Special Forces, but eventually dropped out, perhaps spurring on his later anti-US government attitude.

Derrida makes this claim in his 2001 treatise *On Cosmopolitanism and Forgiveness* (part of the "Thinking in Action" series). He is dealing with the problem of amnesty where the bloody and horrific tragedies of history demand forgiveness.

forgiveness—n. 1 a forgiving or being forgiven; pardon *2* inclination to forgive or pardon.
  "forgiveness." *Webster's New World College Dictionary: Fourth Edition* (Foster City: IDG Books Worldwide, 2000), p. 555.

Page 49

A party thrown by the Kennedys would likely be hosted at the "Kennedy Compound" in the seaside town of Hyannis Port, Massachusetts, on Cape Cod. The estate is located just two miles from the village's downtown area. Thousands of tourists visit its gates each year, but only those invited are permitted inside.

The list of Kennedys who had died tragically at time of writing includes the following (the year and cause of death is found in parentheses): Joseph P. Kennedy Jr. (1944, died flying a bombing mission over Europe in WWII), Kathleen Agnes "Kick" Kennedy (1948, plane crash), Patrick Bouvier Kennedy (1963, complications at birth), John Fitzgerald Kennedy (1963, assassinated in Dallas), Robert F. Kennedy (1968, assassinated in Los Angeles), David Anthony Kennedy (1984, drug overdose), Michael LeMoyne Kennedy (1997, skiing accident), John F. Kennedy Jr. (1999, plane crash), Carolyn Bessette Kennedy (1999, plane crash), and Ted Kennedy (former senator from Massachusetts), who survived two close calls with death—a plane crash in 1964 and a car crash in 1969, in addition to struggles with alcoholism—prior to his death in 2009 from a malignant brain tumor. Since this book's initial release in 2004, additional deaths speculatively linked to the "Kennedy Curse" include Kara Kennedy (2011, heart attack), Mary Richardson Kennedy (2012, suicide), Saoirse Kennedy Hill (2019, drug overdose), and Maeve Kennedy McKean (2020, canoe accident).

Other members of the Kennedy family who maintain public lives and might attend such a party include: Kathleen Kennedy Townsend (former lieutenant governor of Maryland), Maria Shriver (television personality and former first lady of California), Patrick Kennedy (former congressman from Rhode Island), Joseph P. Kennedy II (former congressman from Massachusetts), Robert F. Kennedy Jr. (lawyer and environmental activist turned conspiracy-theory-floating presidential candidate), Kerry Kennedy (human rights activist and ex-wife of Andrew Cuomo), and Rory E. K. Kennedy (documentary filmmaker and social activist).

Page 53

Not only can drug use induce liver damage, but a damaged liver can affect the efficacy of a drug. Fluoxetine, in particular, will be slower to break down in people who have cirrhotic livers. The normal half-life of fluoxetine is 2 to 3 days; in patients with damaged livers, that half-life increases to a mean of 7.6 days.

On May 30, 2001, a 3-judge panel of the Court of Appeals for the Federal Circuit in Washington, DC, reaffirmed its decision (with certain modifications) that Eli Lilly and Company's 2003 patent was invalid due to double patenting.[a] On July 18 of that year, the court turned down the company's request for another appeal, assuring that generic forms of the drug would still be made available.[b]

[a] "Appeals Court Modifies Its Ruling on 2003 Prozac Patent, Company to Seek Legal Review." *BusinessWire.* (May 30, 2001).

[b] "Appeals Court Denies Lilly Petition for Rehearing of Prozac Patent Case; Company To Appeal to United States Supreme Court" *BusinessWire.* (July 18, 2001).

In September of 2001, Eli Lilly and Company introduced PROZAC Weekly, pitched as "the first and only once-a-week medication of its kind." PROZAC Weekly is a product aimed at people who have trouble remembering to consistently take once-a-day medications. Eli Lilly still holds a patent for PROZAC Weekly.

At time of writing, www.prozac.com (now defunct) suggested possible conversation starters for those who wish to discuss PROZAC Weekly with their doctors. Some examples from the website included:

1. Taking a pill every day reminds me that I have depression.
2. I sometimes have down days and wonder if they could be caused by missed medications.
3. I consider my schedule busy.
4. I travel frequently.

Page 54

Health journalist Laurie Tarkan's mother died of a liver disorder when Tarkan was 11 years old.

Tarkan, Laurie. "Many Drugs Harm the Liver, but Most Remain on the Market," *New York Times*, Aug. 14, 2001.

Page 55

Vallejo, César. "Considering coldly, impartially" in *The Complete Posthumous Poetry* (Berkeley: University of California Press, 1978), p. 73.

The Peruvian poet César Vallejo was descended from two Chimu Indian grandmothers and two Catholic priest grandfathers. He was a lifelong political activist. He was particularly moved as a young man, observing the backbreaking labor of underpaid workers on the sugar plantation where he worked in the accounts department. He went on to become a staunch anti-Fascist when he lived in Madrid in his later life.

Page 56

Allergies are the human body's overreaction to substances that it thinks will cause it harm. These include harmless substances such as dust and pollen. Tears are the eyes' attempt to purge themselves of these irritants. This excess activity can often lead to conjunctivitis (pink eye). According to the American Academy of Ophthalmology, 22 million Americans have allergies, and a majority of them have allergic conjunctivitis.

According to the Centers for Disease Control and Prevention (CDC), heart disease is responsible for the deaths of 21.8% American women.

"Leading Causes of Death – Females – All races and origins – United States, 2018." CDC. https://www.cdc.gov/women/lcod/2018/all-races -origins/index.htm.

Haitian immigrant Abner Louima was arrested in front of Club Rendezvous in Brooklyn on Saturday, August 9, 1997. New York City police officers arrested him after dispersing a disorderly crowd out-side the nightclub, reporting that Louima had struck Officer Justin Volpe with his fist. The police officers reportedly beat Louima inside their patrol car. Then later, in the precinct bathroom, witnesses say Officer Charles Schwarz held down Louima while Volpe sodomized him with a broken broomstick. Schwarz served a 5-year jail sentence for perjury, while Volpe pleaded guilty and was sentenced in 1999 to 30 years in prison. Volpe was transferred from a federal correctional facility to community confinement in April 2023, with plans for a full release in 2024. Reached by reporters while under house arrest in Staten Island in summer 2023, Volpe stated, "I have nothing but love in my heart for New York City and everybody in my case involved, especially Mr. Louima."

Grunlund, Maura. "Ex-cop from Staten Island, Justin Volpe, released early from prison for brutal assault of Abner Louima." Staten Island Live, June 14, 2023, https://www.silive.com/crime-safety/2023/06/ex-cop-justin-volpe-convicted-in-brutal-assault-of-abner-louima-now-on-supervised-release-from-prison.html. Accessed August 24, 2023.

Page 57

Amadou Diallo, a West African immigrant and street vendor, was shot dead in the early morning hours of February 4, 1999, in the vestibule of his Bronx apartment building. Despite the fact that Diallo was unarmed, four police officers from the now-disbanded "Street Crime Unit" expended 41 rounds shooting at him. He was declared dead at the scene. In a February 2000 trial, the four officers were acquitted of all charges (including second-degree murder).

The most publicized reaction to the killing of Amadou Diallo was the performance by Bruce Springsteen of his song "American Skin (41 Shots)." He premiered the song at a June 4, 2000, concert in Atlanta. Before the tour reached New York, eight days later, the head of the New York City Police Benevolent Association had already called for all 27,000 New York City police officers to boycott the show and refuse to moonlight as security guards. The Police Commissioner Howard Safir supported him, and Bob Lucente, the president of the state chapter of the Fraternal Order of Police, lost his job over the issue, after saying, "[Springsteen's] turned into some type of fucking dirtbag. He goes on the boycott list. He has all these good songs and everything, American-flag songs and all that

stuff, and now he's a floating fag, and you can quote me on that."
Springsteen's song describes a mother warning her son to always
admit inferiority to police officers, noting that "The secret my friend /
You can get killed just for living in your American skin." This song
was released only as a single, and was not included, to the chagrin
of many critics, on his next full album *The Rising*, which was re-
leased after the events of September 11, 2001, in which many New
York City police officers lost their lives. A studio version of the song
appeared on Springsteen's 2014 album *High Hopes*, and he continues
to play it publicly in dedication to other victims of police violence,
including Trayvon Martin and George Floyd.

Diallo's name continues to be evoked by Black Lives Matter and other
anti-police-violence protest movements.

In Myung Mi Kim's fourth book of poetry *Commons* (Berkeley:
University of California Press, 2002), her final words are the sugges-
tion to "mobilize our notion of the responsibility to one another in
social space."

Page 61
Translator and poet Paul Celan committed suicide in 1970.

"All those sleep shapes" ("Alle die Schlafgestalten") from Celan's final
book *Zeitgehöft*, published in 1976.

Celan, Paul. *Poems of Paul Celan*, trans. Michael Hamburger (New
York: Persea Books, 1988), pp. 336–337.

Page 64
According to a 2001 report from the Centers for Disease Control and
Prevention (using 1999 mortality data), the leading cause of death for
adults, aged 25 or older, in the state of New Hampshire was cardio-
vascular disease (39%).

The name of this café is a reference to a room used for measured coffee tasting. "Cupping" coffee means to sample different coffees to determine their flavor profiles. Cupping is also used to determine if a coffee has defects or in the process of creating new blends. A cupping room, somewhat like a clean room, is a space built with precisely controlled conditions that establish the ideal environment for cupping. The Cupping Room Café's L-shaped design—with windows only at either end—and its oft-open doors does not, in fact, create the requisite conditions for an actual cupping room. Opened in Soho in 1977, the Cupping Room Café closed permanently in 2020, at the height of the COVID-19 crisis.

Page 67

In 1999, 12-year-old Lionel Tate beat his 6-year-old neighbor, Tiffany Eunick, to death, pretending to be a professional wrestler. Prosecutors offered his mother a deal that he spend 3 years in a juvenile facility, which she turned down believing her son would be acquitted. Instead, he was found guilty and sentenced to life in prison without parole, the youngest person ever given such a sentence in the United States. He has received support from the NAACP, the Vatican, and the Human Rights Commission in Geneva, but his request for clemency was left solely in the hands of Florida governor Jeb Bush, who turned down Tate's first request due to his poor conduct in prison. A second request for clemency was entered by Tate's prosecutor, Kenneth Padowitz, who feels his sentence is too harsh, and should have been no more than 6 to 9 months.

Lionel Tate was one of nearly 3,000 juveniles tried as an adult in the state of Florida in 2001.

Lionel's mother, Kathleen Grossett-Tate, is a Florida state trooper.

In December 2003, Lionel Tate's first-degree murder conviction and life prison sentence were overturned by the Florida appellate court, who determined that his mental competency should have been tested before the trial. He was then offered a rare second opportunity to sign a plea bargain by the prosecution. He agreed to a second-degree murder charge that shortened his prison sentence to 3 years—the majority of which he had already served. Both Tate and his mother said they were disappointed by the plea bargain, thinking he was guilty of manslaughter and not murder, but they agreed to the murder charge so he could be granted his freedom.

In January 2004, Tate was released into a year of house arrest and 10 years of probation. In May 2005, Tate returned to prison after holding up a pizza delivery man at gunpoint. In his 2006 trial, he pleaded guilty to parole violation and armed robbery. Sentencing Tate to 30 years in prison, Judge Joel T. Lazarus of the Broward County Circuit Court said, "In plain English, Lionel Tate, you've run out of chances. You do not get any more."

Aguayo, Terry. "Youth Who Killed at 12 Gets 30 Years for Violating Probation." *New York Times*, May 19, 2006, https://www.nytimes.com /2006/05/19/us/19sentence.html. Accessed August 24, 2023.

Page 68

The directions for Tylenol Extra Strength, for children 6–11 years old, states: "Do not use this adult Extra Strength product in children under 12 years of age; this will provide more than the recommended dose (overdose) of Tylenol and could cause serious health problems." Lionel would have been permitted to "take 2 tablets, caplets, gelcaps or geltabs every 4 to 6 hours as needed," once he entered the correction center. Though, presumably, personnel at the infirmary would have prevented him from taking "more than 8 tablets, caplets, gelcaps or geltabs in 24 hours."

Page 71

On July 2, 2001, Robert "Bob" Tools of Franklin in south-central Kentucky received an artificial heart. Residents of the 8,000-person town were surprised to find this out when the press descended on Franklin that day. Most people were familiar with the gregarious Tools, but did not know he was the first to undergo such a revolutionary surgery. "I don't see how they kept it secret that long," said barber Clay Kinnard, 71. Still, residents said they were impressed but would honor Tools's privacy and give him the necessary solitude needed to convalesce.

Shipley, Sara. "Folks in Franklin Remained Unaware or Carefully Quiet." *The Courier-Journal*, August 22, 2001.

Seventy-three days after Tools received his artificial heart, Tom Christerson of Central City, Kentucky, became the second patient to have the experimental AbioCor pump implanted in his chest. The 70-year-old was operated on by University of Louisville surgeons, as Tools was.

Tools, 59, died on November 30, 2001, almost five months after receiving his artificial heart. He died of severe abdominal bleeding, which doctors did not attribute to the AbioCor pump, but said that it was more likely caused by blood thinners he needed to take to aid the performance of the implant.

Christerson died in 2003 at the age of 71, 17 months after receiving the implant. Abiomed, the company which manufactured the AbiCor, stated that Christerson died after a membrane on the artificial heart wore out.

"Family, Friends Say Goodbye to Heart Pioneer Tom Christerson." WAVE News, February 11, 2003, https://www.wave3.com/story/1125178/family-friends-say-goodbye-to-heart-pioneer-tom-christerson/. Accessed August 22, 2023.

Page 72
South African writer John Maxwell (J. M.) Coetzee was awarded the 2003 Nobel Prize in literature.

White Teeth is Zadie Smith's debut novel, published in June 2001 when she was 23 years old.

Coetzee's novel *Disgrace* won the 1999 Booker Prize, making him the first writer to win the award twice (*The Life and Times of Michael K* won in 1983).

According to the South African Truth and Reconciliation Commission (TRC), it "was set up by the Government of National Unity to help deal with what happened under apartheid. The conflict during this period resulted in violence and human rights abuses from all sides. No section of society escaped these abuses." The TRC was established by the Promotion of National Unity and Reconciliation Act, No. 34 of 1995. Nelson Mandela was a particular supporter of the TRC. Those critical of the Commission, including members of Mandela's own African National Congress, feel that the committee is too lenient, offering amnesty to whites who admit to killing Blacks during apartheid.

naturalism—n. Literature, Art, etc. a) faithful adherence to nature; realism; specif., the principles and methods of a group of 19th-cent. writers, including Emile Zola, Gustave Flaubert, and Guy de Maupassant, who believed that the writer or artist should apply scientific objectivity and precision in observing and depicting life, without idealizing, imposing value judgments, or avoiding what may be regarded as sordid or repulsive. *b)* the quality resulting from the use of such realism.
   "naturalism." *Webster's New World College Dictionary: Fourth Edition* (Foster City: IDG Books Worldwide, 2000), p. 960.

petrous—adj. of or like rock; hard; stony.
   "petrous." *Webster's New World College Dictionary: Fourth Edition* (Foster City: IDG Books Worldwide, 2000), p. 1077.

A search on Google for the keywords "rape" and "statistics" on November 17, 2003, at 8:22 p.m., followed by the command "I'm Feeling Lucky" turned up a website entitled "RAINN Statistics." RAINN is the Rape, Abuse & Incest National Network. According to RAINN, 14.8% of American women have been victims of completed rape and another 2.8% victims of attempted rape (approximately 1 in 6 women, all told).

Page 74

A "Between the Sheets" calls for one part brandy, one part white rum, one part triple sec, and a dash of lemon juice. Shake ingredients together with ice, then strain into a cocktail glass. Garnish with lemon peel and serve.

Page 77

Diflucan is an oral tablet.

The first warning that the drug company Pfizer lists on its description of Diflucan is as follows: "(1) Hepatic injury: DIFLUCAN has been associated with rare cases of serious hepatic toxicity, including fatalities primarily in patients with serious underlying medical conditions. In cases of DIFLUCAN-associated hepatotoxicity, no obvious relationship to total daily dose, duration of therapy, sex or age of the patient has been observed. DIFLUCAN hepatotoxicity has usually, but not always, been reversible on discontinuation of therapy. Patients who develop abnormal liver function tests during DIFLUCAN therapy should be monitored for the development of more severe hepatic injury. DIFLUCAN should be discontinued if clinical signs and symptoms consistent with liver disease develop that may be attributable to DIFLUCAN." This is the only warning printed in bold.

Davidson, Adam. "Working Stiffs: The Necessary Parasites of Capitalism." *Harper's Magazine* (August 2001), pp. 48–54.

Page 81

On February 13, 2002, Queen Elizabeth II granted Rudolph Giuliani honorary knighthood for his role following the September 11, 2001, terrorist attacks on New York City. An honorary Knighthood of the British Empire, an order which dates back to 1917, is an honor bestowed by the Crown of England to non-British citizens. The bestowing of his title did not include a dubbing ceremony in which he knelt before the Queen as she touched his shoulder with a sword, and Giuliani was not obligated to fight in defense of Great Britain, although he did receive a medal. (He was also not permitted the title "Sir," although he was permitted to sign the letters "K.B.E."—along with the "Esq." that his law degree permits him—after his name.)

In September 2021, following Queen Elizabeth II's comments commemorating the 20th anniversary of the attacks, Giulani falsely claimed that he had turned down the honorary knighthood, on the (inaccurate) grounds that he would have been required to renounce his American citizenship. Speaking in New York at a commemorative dinner at Cipriani's, Giuliani (apparently imitating the Queen) said, "You did a wonderful job on September 11, and therefore I am making you an honorable Knight Commander of the . . . royal something or other."

Hoffman, Jordan. "Rudy Giuliani Finds New Way to Disgrace Himself by Insulting Queen Elizabeth." *Vanity Fair* (September 12, 2021), https://www.vanityfair.com/style/2021/09/rudy-giuliani-finds-new-way-to-disgrace-himself-by-insulting-queen-elizabeth. Accessed August 25, 2023.

Sean Connery, who passed away in 2020 at the age of 90, being Scottish, had his knighthood bestowed upon him on July 5, 2000, in Edinburgh. He said it was "one of the proudest days of his life." His knighthood was particularly controversial given his Scottish separatist views. Connery reportedly gave £4,800 a month to the Scottish National Party. This association caused his bid for knighthood to be denied on two previous occasions. Many Scottish nationalists felt Connery's acceptance of knighthood was a betrayal to the cause.

Stage and screen actor John Gielgud, a publicly acknowledged homosexual, was granted knighthood in 1953. Many felt he deserved the title earlier in his life, and he did finally receive it after fellow actors and knights, Laurence Olivier and Ralph Richardson, pleaded with Prime Minister Winston Churchill to correct the situation.

On June 15, 2002, the Rolling Stones' lead singer Mick Jagger was made a knight at the official birthday celebration of Queen Elizabeth II. He was the fourth rock 'n' roll artist to be given this honor, following the Beatles' Paul McCartney, singer-songwriter Elton John, and Irishman, Boomtown Rats singer, and Live Aid impresario, Bob Geldof.

From Wallace Stevens's speech "The Noble Rider and the Sound of Words," first published by the Princeton University Press in 1942. The speech addresses his own and other poets' removal from political concerns in their work. He suggests that such poets play a greater social role than those contemporary poets who create politically didactic verse.

Page 84

Georg Wilhelm Friedrich Hegel puts forth this concept in his "Philosophy of Right."

Antigone, daughter of Oedipus, was a member of the cursed house of Thebes. Her brother Polynices opposed Creon, their uncle and King of Thebes, to whom Oedipus had voluntarily passed his crown. Creon then turned on Oedipus and expelled him from Thebes. After defeating Polynices, Creon declared, as law, that it was illegal to bury his body. Antigone gave her brother a proper and respectful interment and then presented herself to Creon without fear; she had already forfeited her own life the moment she decided to bury her brother. Right before she was executed she said, "Behold me, what I suffer / Because I have upheld that which is high."

In the decade following September 11, 2001, reports periodically emerged speculating that Osama bin Laden had been killed, usually as a result of US bombing raids in Afghanistan. Reports also periodically appeared describing bin Laden sightings or evidence of his communications. Public response to both types of reports seemed to lessen with each one, increasingly bringing forth the question of whether bin Laden's physical survival was important at all. Bin Laden's actual death would not be confirmed until President Obama announced—in a live broadcast from the White House—that bin Laden had been killed during a US-led operation in Pakistan on May 2, 2011.

Page 85

Officially titled "Nowhere to Run," this parody by Madblast was published on the now-defunct website politicaltoons.com (and widely shared by email) following the September 11 attacks. The video included a cartoon version of Colin Powell singing "Daylight come and we drop-a de bomb," as an animated photo of bin Laden scampers between missiles. Archival copies of the video are still widely available on YouTube.

Madblast. "Bin Laden Has Nowhere to Run—Nowhere to Hide." politicaltoons.com/osama.cfm. Accessed 2004. See also https://www.youtube.com/watch?v=ROJ7w2yBd1l. Accessed August 23, 2023.

Boxer, Sarah, "Point, Click and Mock on the Wild, Wild Web." *New York Times*, October 21, 2004, https://www.nytimes.com/2004/10/21/arts/point-click-and-mock-on-the-wild-wild-web.html. Accessed August 23, 2023.

Page 89

The West Side Highway, which runs along the Hudson River on New York's West Side, becomes the Henry Hudson Parkway as it enters Riverside Park at 66th Street. The Henry Hudson Parkway continues through Harlem and crosses from Manhattan's northernmost point into the Bronx. Once it crosses into Westchester County it becomes the Saw Mill Parkway and brings motorists to upstate New York's scenic Hudson Valley. The Saw Mill, one of America's earliest four-lane roads, is more reminiscent of Robert Moses's original concept of parkways established for lazy Sunday drives, as opposed to more modern superhighways established for the purpose of getting people and cargo as fast as possible from one metropolitan center to another. Were one to take the West Side Highway downtown, to the southern tip of Manhattan, one could enter the Brooklyn Battery Tunnel, go under the East River, and get on the Belt Parkway in

Brooklyn. The Belt Parkway goes east on Long Island and, once it crosses into Nassau County, becomes the Southern State Parkway. The traffic on these roads, particularly in the summer, is evidence of Moses's grand plan gone awry.

Columbia University is located uptown in the Morningside Heights neighborhood. The center of the campus, on Broadway and 116th Street, is about 3 blocks from the Henry Hudson Highway, if you were to cut through Riverside Park.

Page 90
The full name of the Islamic fundamentalist group commonly referred to as al Qaeda is "al-Qaeda al-Sulbah," which means "The Solid Base." In the organization's founding charter, it is described as the "spearhead of Islam" and the "pioneering vanguard of the Islamic movements."

Page 92
Founded in 1982, with an IPO in 1996, eTrade was a flagship online stock-trading platform. The company was acquired by Morgan Stanley for $13 billion in 2020.

Originating in a trademark advertising slogan by the Eastman Kodak Company (which was a dominant camera and film producer through most of the 20th century), a "Kodak moment" originally implied a precious, fleeting instant that deserved to be captured forever on film. Beginning in the 1990s, the company struggled to stay current with the rise of digital photography—so much so that the phrase "a Kodak moment" was also ironically used to describe a business's failure to keep pace with technical innovation. Eastman Kodak declared bankruptcy in 2013, eventually emerging from the proceedings with a much-narrowed focus on software for commercial printers.

Ziboro, Paul. "So, What Does Kodak Do These Days?" *Wall Street Journal*, August 7, 2020, https://www.wsj.com/articles/what-does-kodak-do-these-days-a-decade-of-pivots-before-a-huge-federal-loan-11596806449. Accessed August 23, 2023.

"I am Tiger Woods" was the slogan associated with Nike's 1997 print-and broadcast-advertising campaign featuring the wunderkind professional golf champion.

In the September 11, 2001, attack, not only were the Twin Towers destroyed, but the whole system of buildings that surrounded and connected them, known as the "World Trade Center Complex."

Condoleezza Rice on President George W. Bush—"He least likes me to say, 'This is complex.'" See Nicholas Lemann's "Without a Doubt" in the *New Yorker*, (October 14, 2002).

Page 93

The USA Patriot Act was passed by the United States House of Representatives on October 24, 2001. The full title of the legislation is the "Uniting and Strengthening America by Providing Appropriate Tools Required to Intercept and Obstruct Terrorism Act of 2001." Two days later, President Bush signed it into law. This 342-page document was drafted and passed in a hurry following the terrorist activities of September 11. It gives substantial new power to both domestic law-enforcement groups and international intelligence agencies in pursuing terrorists, allowing them to bypass the usual checks and balances provided by the judicial branch of the government. While several provisions are set to expire, others are not, including giving the government the right to subpoena electronic communications, an override of the privacy provisions of the Cable Act for communication services offered by cable providers, and "Sneak and Peek" allowances, which lets law enforcement delay notification of the execution of a warrant. In November 2003, the FBI invoked the Patriot Act to subpoena financial documents to aid them in uncovering a political corruption scandal involving a Las Vegas strip club. This was the first obvious use of the Patriot Act in a non-terrorism-related matter. In early 2003, a draft of the Justice Department's follow-up bill, "The Domestic Security Enhancement Act of 2003," was leaked to the press by the nonpartisan Center for Public Integrity, a civil rights group. This act was dubbed "Patriot II." Though it received criticism and was shelved, some points have been advanced through other legislation.

Page 95

According to the Centers for Disease Control and Prevention (CDC), the first case of inhalation anthrax attack in the United States was reported in Palm Beach County, Florida,[a] on October 4, 2001. The 63-year-old Robert Stevens was probably exposed to the anthrax on September 19, opening mail in his office at America Media in Boca Raton. He began showing signs of illness on September 30 and died on October 5.

[a] Palm Beach County was the focus of national attention the previous year as the site of a vote recount in the 2000 presidential election.

Stevens was the first of 5 people to be killed in a series of anthrax attacks between September 18 and October 12, 2001. (22 people, including 12 mail handlers, were seriously sickened.) While the culprit for the attacks remained at large for several years, the FBI investigation ultimately centered on Bruce Edwards Ivins, a biodefense researcher at the Army Medical Research Institute of Infectious Diseases in Fort Detrick, MD. Ivins, 62, committed suicide on July 29, 2008, as federal prosecutors were preparing to present their investigation to a grand jury. Before taking a lethal overdose of Tylenol, Ivins wrote a note reading, "Please let me sleep. Please."

The CDC's list of symptoms for inhalation anthrax includes fever and chills; chest discomfort; shortness of breath; confusion or dizziness; cough; nausea, vomiting, or stomach pains; headache; sweats (often drenching); extreme tiredness; and body aches.

Broughton, Ashley. "'Let me sleep,' anthrax suspect wrote before suicide." CNN, January 6, 2009, https://www.cnn.com/2009/CRIME/01/06/anthrax.ivins/. Accessed August 24, 2023.

"Symptoms of Anthrax." Centers for Disease Control and Prevention, November 20, 2020, https://www.cdc.gov/anthrax/symptoms/index.html. Accessed August 24, 2023.

Page 99

Mahalia Jackson was gospel music's first superstar and is still generally considered the greatest gospel singer ever. She is noted for her crossover success, creating music that appealed to an ever-expanding audience over the course of her career, solidified by her appearance at the Newport Jazz Festival in 1958.

George Wein was a Boston-born jazz pianist who launched his own career at the Newport Jazz Festival, in 1954. He also opened the notable jazz club, Storyville.

Mahalia Jackson performed her farewell concert in Germany in 1971, just months before she died.

Paul Celan made this statement during his speech on the occasion of being awarded the Bremen Prize for German Literature (the Literature Prize of the Free Hanseatic City of Bremen) in 1958. He said that language must be freed from history.

Page 100

Mahalia Jackson faced particular adversity in the later years of her life. Her friends and fellow civil rights activists Martin Luther King Jr., John F. Kennedy, and Robert F. Kennedy were all assassinated, causing her to retire from political life in 1968. She then went through a notably messy and well-publicized divorce that led to her physical deterioration; she had several heart attacks and lost a hundred pounds quite quickly. Still, she was able to regain her form and perform several concerts before dying on January 27, 1972.

André Breton also cites this passage from Hegel in his Surrealist novel *Nadja*.

Page 102

The novelist and playwright Sarah Schulman told this story.

The fact that Frieda Berger had such a tattoo at all was enough to signify that she had been imprisoned at Auschwitz. Auschwitz Concentration Camp complex was the only site where prisoners were systemically tattooed during the Holocaust. A more common practice was having serial numbers sewn into the clothing of inmates. The tattooing at Auschwitz began in 1941 when about 12,000 Soviet prisoners of war were brought there. In May of 1944, the "A" series was introduced (the previous system used no letter prefixes except for Soviets [AU], Gypsies [Z], and those slated for "reeducation" [EH]). "A" actually signified nothing more than the beginning of the alphabet. The "A" series was to be given to the first 20,000 new Jewish male prisoners and the first 20,000 new Jewish female prisoners. Subsequent series were to follow the alphabet, but the camps were closed before the "B" series was completed. Due to a logistical error, the "A" series for women was assigned to 25,378 prisoners before the "B" series was begun.

> Rosenthal, George. "The Evolution of Tattooing in the Auschwitz Concentration Camp Complex." jewishvirtuallibrary.org/the -evolution-of-tatooing-in-the-auschwitz-concentration-camp -complex.

Page 103

On April 2, 2002, Israeli Prime Minister Ariel Sharon (1928–2014, in office 2001–2008) suggested that Palestinian Authority leader Yasser Arafat (1929–2004, in office 1994–2004) be sent from the Gaza Strip and the West Bank and into exile.

US Secretary of State Colin Powell responded to Sharon's suggestion in April 2002 negatively, saying Arafat "still has a role to play." Following the January 5, 2003, double-suicide bombing in Tel Aviv, Sharon once again announced his intention to expel Arafat, once American actions in Iraq had concluded.

A survivor of multiple assassination attempts, Arafat lived from 2001 to 2004 in the ruins of the presidential headquarters in Ramallah, surrounded by the Israeli Army. In October 2004, after reporting stomach pains, he was flown to a French military hospital outside Paris, where he ultimately died of a stroke on November 11. His death sparked many conspiracy theories, including that Arafat had died of AIDS complications. His widow, Suha, maintains that he was poisoned with plutonium by Israel. Following an official investigation, a French court in 2015 ruled out foul play.

Agent France-Presse in Nanterre. "France closes Yasser Arafat murder inquiry with no charges brought." *The Guardian*, September 2, 2015, https://www.theguardian.com/world/2015/sep/02/yasser-arafat-murder -investigation-closed-france. Accessed August 23, 2023.

Arafat is discussed as a place of forgiveness in the Koran. Line 175 of Surah Al-Baqarah (Surah 2. The Cow—Day Two) reads, "They are the ones who buy Error in place of Guidance and Torment in place of Forgiveness. Ah! what boldness (They show) for the Fire!" Lines 198 and 199 read, "It is no crime in you if ye seek of the bounty of your Lord (during pilgrimage). Then when ye pour down from (Mount) Arafat, celebrate the praises of Allah at the Sacred Monument, and celebrate His praises as He has directed you, even though, before this, ye went astray. Then pass on at a quick pace from the place whence it is usual for the multitude so to do, and ask for Allah's forgiveness. For Allah is Oft-forgiving, Most Merciful."

Page 107

This 1937 film featured Katharine Hepburn and Ginger Rogers as stage actresses who lived together in a boarding house. The film is remarkably moving for a primarily comedic movie. It was notable for its female-dominant cast that also included Lucille Ball, Eve Arden, and Ann Miller. *Stage Door* was nominated for three Academy Awards: Best Picture, Best Director, and Best Screenplay.

Page 108

On April 15, 2002, the FDA approved Botox for the use in removing or lessening the appearance of frown lines. Allergan, Inc. first introduced the product in 1989 to treat certain serious eye-muscle disorders.

Enron's official company description, November 2003, when Enron was in the midst of restructuring various businesses for distribution as ongoing companies to its creditors and liquidating its remaining operations.

Page 109

Bottled-water sales in the United States rose 9.3% in 2000 to $5.7 billion, according to Beverage Marketing Corporation, a New York-based research and consulting firm: www.bottledwaterweb.com.

Page 109–111

In the wake of the September 11, 2001, attacks, airports were particularly strapped for cash, not only due to the marked drop in air travel but because of the exorbitant costs for increased security. For instance, John Wayne Airport in Orange County, California, estimated spending an additional $1 million per month on security and at the Hartsfield International Airport in Atlanta, security costs increased by $2 million per month.

Page 111

Severe acute respiratory syndrome (SARS) is a viral respiratory illness. SARS was first reported in Asia in February 2003. Over the next few months, the illness spread to more than two dozen countries in North America, South America, Europe, and Asia. The SARS global outbreak of 2003 was eventually contained; however, scientists noted that it was possible that the disease could reemerge.

In general, SARS begins with a high fever (temperature greater than 100.4°F). The main way that SARS seems to spread is by close person-to-person contact. In the context of SARS, close contact means having cared for or lived with someone with SARS or having direct contact with respiratory secretions or body fluids of a patient with SARS. Examples of close contact include kissing or hugging, sharing eating or drinking utensils, talking to someone within 3 feet, and touching someone directly. Close contact does not include activities like walking by a person or sitting across a waiting room or office for a brief time.

"SARS Basic Fact Sheet." Centers for Disease Control and Prevention, 2003, https://www.cdc.gov/sars/about/fs-sars.html. Accessed August 23, 2023.

In February 2020, the World Health Organization (WHO) announced that the novel coronavirus which had begun circulating in 2019 would be officially named "severe acute respiratory syndrome coronavirus 2 (SARS-CoV-2)," and that the disease caused by this virus would be called "coronavirus disease of 2019 (COVID-19)." According to the WHO, "This name was chosen because the virus is genetically related to the coronavirus responsible for the SARS outbreak of 2003. While related, the two viruses are different."

The National Institutes of Health noted in July 2020 that SARS-CoV-2 is "less deadly but far more contagious" than its 2003 predecessor. After declaring in March 2020 that SARS-CoV-2 was not capable of airborne transmission, the WHO eventually amended this conclusion after advocacy by scientists and medical professionals. In April 2021, the WHO issued an official update, advising that in addition to spread by close contact, "The virus can also spread in poorly ventilated and/ or crowded indoor settings, where people tend to spend longer periods of time. This is because aerosols remain suspended in the air or travel farther than 1 metre (long-range)."

Chamary, JV. "WHO Finally Admits Coronavirus Is Airborne. It's Too Late." *Forbes*, May 4, 2021, https://www.forbes.com/sites/jvchamary /2021/05/04/who-coronavirus-airborne/?sh=874f4324472c. Accessed August 23, 2023.

Petersen, Eskild, et al. "Comparing SARS-CoV-2 with SARS-CoV and influenza pandemics." *Lancet*, vol. 20, no. 9, 2020, pp. e238-e244. PubMed Central, https://doi.org/10.1016/S1473-3099(20)30484-9.

World Health Organization. "Naming the coronavirus disease (COVID-19) and the virus that causes it." Country & Technical Guidance – Coronavirus disease (COVID-19), July 17, 2020, https://www.who.int/emergencies/diseases/novel-coronavirus-2019/technical-guidance. Accessed August 23, 2023.

Page 113

The longest Marlboros available are either Marlboro Light 100's Superlong or Marlboro Red 100's Superlong.

On January 27, 2003, Philip Morris Companies, Inc. changed its corporate moniker to Altria Group, Inc. This is a parent company that includes Kraft Foods, Inc., Philip Morris International, Inc., and Philip Morris USA, Inc. The company retained the Philip Morris brand name for its cigarette products. According to an Altria press release, "The Altria name and logo powerfully express these enduring qualities: its drive toward excellence, its companies' focus on building brands, its passion for success, its openness to innovation, its commitment to its communities and societies, and its focus on its people." The word "Altria" has no etymological source. According to a University of California, San Francisco study published in the *American Journal of Public Health*, the company's name change was a public relations effort to divorce itself from its reputation as primarily a tobacco company without actually hurting its sales in those divisions. The study says that the company has diverted attention away from the reason for the name change because a consumer association of Altria with tobacco would cause the maneuver to fail. Altria will not promote any of its tobacco products on the Internet and will only provide advertisement if requested by email. Philip Morris International and Altria formally split in 2008 while facing mounting legal pressure in the US. Since then, Philip Morris International has handled the marketing and sale of Marlboro-branded products abroad while investing substantially in alternative tobacco devices including e-cigarettes and vape pens. In 2023, the company announced its intentions to become a "majority smoke-free company" by 2025, noting $10.7 billion cumulative dollars invested in smoke-free products since 2008.

"Philip Morris International Releases Integrated Report 2022." Philip Morris International, April 5, 2023, https://www.pmi.com/investor -relations/press-releases-and-events/press-releases-overview/press -release-details/?newsId=26266. Accessed August 24, 2023.

Johnston, Ian and Massoudi, Arash. "Philip Morris rules out future merger with Altria." *Financial Times*, November 9, 2021, https://www .ft.com/content/bebc116d-f2ad-49b7-83a4-8bc1b3cc798a. Accessed August 24, 2023.

Juicy Fruit gum has had one of the longest-running sustained advertising campaigns. Its "The taste is gonna move ya!" campaign began in 1983.

Director of *Secrets and Lies*, Englishman Mike Leigh is noted for his ability to take subjects for his films that on paper appear to risk over-the-top melodrama, but with his understated style come off as subtle movies focused on personal interactions.

Page 117

Operation Iraqi Freedom was the official name used by the US government for American military action conducted in Iraq between March 2003 and November 2011. The name is related to Operation Enduring Freedom, which, under the umbrella of the Global War on Terror, refers to 2001–2014 US military action targeting the removal of the Taliban regime in Afghanistan and the elimination of al Qaeda. (The US Department of Veterans Affairs notes that Operation Enduring Freedom was originally called "Operation Infinite Justice.") The Taliban reseized control of Afghanistan in August 2021.

"Veterans Employment Toolkit: Dates and Names of Conflicts." US Department of Veterans Affairs, July 7, 2021, https://www.va.gov /vetsinworkplace/docs/em_datesnames.asp. Accessed August 24, 2023.

The Turkish Parliament disallowed the US military to use its border with Iraq as a staging area during Operation Iraqi Freedom, but then reversed its decision, demanding more aid from the United States.

A statement made by President George W. Bush on April 11, 2003.

Page 118

The tradition of displaying a yellow ribbon as a wish for US troops to return home safely was inspired by the Brown and Levine-penned song "Tie a Yellow Ribbon 'Round the Ole Oak Tree," made popular by Tony Orlando and Dawn with their rendition released in 1971.

Sales of American flags skyrocketed in the immediate aftermath of the September 11 attacks, with Walmart noting it had sold 450,000 flags between September 11 and 13, compared to 26,000 during the same period in the prior year.

"Sales spike for red, white, and blue." CNN, https://www.cnn.com/2001 /US/09/14/flag.sales/index.html.

Page 119–120

Morrison, Toni. "Unspeakable Things Unspoken: The Afro-American Presence in American Literature."

Pharmaceutical applicants against the government of South Africa: Case Number 4183/98.

Page 121

Thabo Mbeki served as Nelson Mandela's deputy president, and had such an active role that Mandela himself referred to him as the "de facto president" of South Africa. The trained economist succeeded Mandela as president in June 1999. Mbeki has been criticized both by Black groups in South Africa for his harsh economic policies and by white groups for his strong affirmative action stance. He is seen as an impressive, if somewhat stiff, intellectual, noted for his British education and signature pipe smoking. His public image is a stark contrast to the charismatic demeanor of his predecessor.

Mandela's HIV T-shirt was given to him by a patient in the Khayelitsha clinic. The former president wore the shirt in support of the distribution of antiretroviral drugs.

Researchers at the Harvard T. H. Chan School of Public Health have estimated that Mbeki's reluctant HIV/AIDS policies resulted in the premature deaths of over 330,000 people between 2000 and 2005, in addition to 35,000 congenital cases. Mbeki has continued to publicly espouse HIV/AIDS skepticism, including in a September 2022 speech for students, diplomats, and members of the media at the University of South Africa.

Gontsana, Mary-Anne. "Treatment Action Campaign admonishes Thabo Mbeki over HIV views following speech." *Daily Maverick South Africa*, September 28, 2022, https://www.dailymaverick.co.za/article/2022-09-28-treatment-action-campaign-admonishes-thabo-mbeki-over-hiv-views-following-speech/. Accessed August 24, 2023.

Power, Samantha. "Letter From South Africa: The AIDS Rebel." *New Yorker* (May 19, 2003), p. 65.

Roeder, Amy. "The cost of South Africa's misguided AIDS policies." Harvard T. H. Chan School of Public Health News, Spring 2009, https://www.hsph.harvard.edu/news/magazine/spr09aids/. Accessed August 24, 2023.

Page 122

Shakespeare, William. *The Tragedy of King Lear* (New York: Signet, 1998), p. 31.

Page 124

Levinas, Emmanuel. "The Transcendence of Words." 1949. *The Levinas Reader*. ed. Seán Hand (Oxford: Blackwell, 1989), pp. 144–49.

Page 125

The Matrix Reloaded (2003, dir. Lana and Lilly Wachowski) disappointed fans and critics alike. Instead of using its pop-cultural façade to reveal its headier philosophical underpinnings, as in the first film (which even inspired a rash of college courses following its release in 1999), the sequel seemed to be a patchwork of action-for-the-sake-of-action sequences and thinly veiled Biblical and mythological references. *The Matrix Reloaded*, separated from its predecessor by four years and a national tragedy, did little to reveal any truths below its flashy surface.

Page 126

There has been an American tradition of professional mourners, particularly common among the new immigrant Irish and Italian communities of the early 20th century. The grieving family would pay a woman to cry at the graveside while the body was interred. In the Irish culture, these professional mourners are called "keeners."

A professional mourner in Korea was the subject of the acclaimed 2002 film *Cry Woman*.

Page 127

Night sweats, or nocturnal sweating, is not actually a sleep disorder in itself but a symptom of some other problem. The most common cause of night sweats is menopause (or andropause in men). Other causes include HIV, tuberculosis, diabetes, sleep apnea, drugs, alcohol, and spicy foods. It is recommended that people suffering from night sweats take a cold shower before bed or during the night when they are awoken by the condition.

On Saturday, December 13, 2003, 600 troops, members of the US 4th Infantry Division and special forces, conducted a "Red Dawn" sweep in the village of Ad Dawr, outside Saddam Hussein's hometown of Tikrit in northern Iraq. They sought a man identified only as a "High Value Target" or HVT. Tucked in a small crawl space ("a spider hole") beneath a metal lean-to in a field, they discovered an unkempt and addled Saddam Hussein. Following his capture, Hussein was tried for crimes against humanity by the Iraqi Interim Government. After a 3-year trial, he was convicted on November 5, 2006, and sentenced to death by hanging. On December 30, 2006—the first day of Eid al-Adha—Hussein was executed before dawn at Camp Justice, a military base in the suburbs of Baghdad.

Page 131

According to a study published in the January 6, 2004, issue of *Annals of Internal Medicine*, "heavy" coffee consumption (six or more cups a day) may help prevent the onset of type 2 diabetes. "We found that heavy coffee consumption substantially reduced the risk of type 2 diabetes in both men and women," said Dr. Frank Hu of the Harvard School of Public Health. The study found men's risk could be reduced by up to 50%, and women by up to 30%. Dr. Peter Martin, the head of the Institute for Coffee Studies at Vanderbilt University, supported this claim, pointing out that there is much more to coffee than just caffeine. Dr. Hu did point out that these findings should not be interpreted as a prescription to drink 6 cups of coffee a day. Numerous subsequent studies have confirmed a link between coffee consumption and a lower risk of type 2 diabetes onset, but, according to a 2023 study in *Clinical Nutrition*, "the mechanism remains unclear."

Berman, Robby. "How coffee helps lower type 2 diabetes risk: New clues on mechanism." *Medical News Today*, March 27, 2023, https://www.medicalnewstoday.com/articles/new-research-reveals-a-potential-mechanism-for-how-coffee-may-reduce-the-risk-of-type-2-diabetes. Accessed August 24, 2023.

On Thursday, August 14, 2003, dozens of cities in the eastern United States and Canada, including New York City, were struck with a major power outage. At 4:10 p.m. EST, 21 power plants in the Niagara region shut down in less than 3 minutes. The New York metro area was one of the last places to have power restored, beginning with the functioning of the Long Island power grid at 9:30 the following night. American and Canadian authorities both attributed the blackout to causes originating on the other side of their shared border.

In the 2004 presidential election, President George W. Bush (R) defeated then-Senator John Kerry (D) by 31 electoral votes. (Bush also took the popular vote, with 50.7% compared to Kerry's 48.3%.)

Page 132

Howe, Fanny. *Tis of Thee* (Berkeley: Atelos, 2003).

Page 133

Elizabeth Costello is the title character of J. M. Coetzee's 2003 novel (his first published subsequent to winning the Booker Prize in 1999 and the Nobel Prize for Literature in 2003). She is an aging novelist who is struggling with a writer's greatest fear, a loss for words.

Coetzee, J. M. *Elizabeth Costello* (New York: Viking Press, 2003), pp. 76–77.

Page 134

Paul Celan's self-description as "Your truly lonely Paul Celan" is from a January 1970 letter written four months before his suicide by drowning.

Celan, Paul. *Collected Prose*, trans. Rosmarie Waldrop (New York: The Sheep Meadow Press, 2003), p. 26.

Page 135

According to the *Oxford English Dicitonary*:

Our contemporary understanding of the word "here," as in "this place" or "the place," finds its origins in the Gothic prefix "hi," meaning this (it is placed before a noun). The pronouns "he," "him," "his," and "her" also come from this source, as well as the pronouns "hither" and "hence." From this source the feminine "she," plural "they," and neuter "it" all eventually evolved.

Images

p. 8 © John Lucas

p. 9 © Shutterstock

p. 15 © John Lucas

p. 17 © John Lucas

p. 18 © John Lucas

p. 21 http://texasnaacp.org/jasper.htm

p. 22 http://texasnaacp.org/jasper,htm

p. 22 © Reuters

p. 25 © Shutterstock

p. 29 © John Lucas

p. 30 © Shutterstock

p. 32 © John Lucas

p. 39 © Liba Taylor/Corbis Historical/Getty Images

p. 40 © John Lucas

p. 42 © John Lucas

p. 43 © Movie Store Collection Ltd/Alamy Stock Photo

p. 47 © Associated Press

p. 55 © John Lucas

p. 56 © Reuters

p. 57 © The Amadou Diallo Foundation, Inc.

p. 62 © John Lucas

p. 67 © Associated Press

p. 68 © John Lucas

p. 70 NIH

p. 71 Mike Simons/Getty Images News

p. 73 © Google

p. 82 © John Lucas

p. 83 © John Lucas

p. 85 Madblast

p. 91 © John Lucas

p. 92 © John Lucas

p. 94 USPS

p. 99 © Leigh A. Wiener

p. 102 © Zbigniew Kosc

p. 118 © John Lucas

p. 121 © Eric Miller/MSF

p. 137 © John Lucas

Grateful acknowledgment is made to the editors of the publications in which poems from this book first appeared: *Boston Review*, *EPR*, *Fence*, *Pierogi*, and *TriQuarterly*.

Grateful acknowledgment is also made to Catherine Barnett, Robert Duffley, John Lucas, and John Woods without whom this book would not be complete.

I would also like to thank Calvin Bedient, Mei-mei Berssenbrugge, Sarah Blake, Allison Coudert, Ulla Dydo, Louise Glück, Polly Gottesman, Saskia Hamilton, Bob Hass, Lyn Hejinian, Christine Hume, Ann Scott Knight, Sabrina Mark, Sarah Schulman, and Mike Goodman for turning this work into a conversation. Thanks also to MacDowell.

Claudia Rankine is the author of six other books, including *Just Us: An American Conversation* and *Citizen: An American Lyric*, which was a *New York Times* best seller and winner of the National Book Critics Circle Award, the Los Angeles Times Book Prize, the Forward Prize, and many other awards. In 2016, Rankine cofounded the Racial Imaginary Institute (TRII). She is a MacArthur Fellow and professor of creative writing at New York University.

claudiarankine.com

The text of *Don't Let Me Be Lonely* is set in Imperial BT.
Book design by John Lucas.
Composition by John Lucas and Bookmobile Design & Digital
Publisher Services, Minneapolis, Minnesota.
Manufactured by Versa Press on acid-free paper.